yt11

26.7.07

CREATIVE OUTDOOR WORK WITH YOUNG PEOPLE

Written and illustrated by

Alan Smith

Russell House Publishing Ltd

D1340403

First published in 1994 by

Russell House Publishing Limited
38 Silver Street
Lyme Regis
Dorset
DT7 3HS

Portions of this book were originally published by the I.T. Resource Centre in 1987 as *Working Out Of Doors With Young People*

British Library Cataloguing-in-Publication Data:
A catalogue record for this book is available from the British Library.

ISBN: 1-898924-25-2

Typeset by:
Enabler Publication Services
3 Russell House
Lym Close
Lyme Regis
Dorset
DT7 3DE

Printed by:
WM Print, Walsall

CONTENTS

INTRODUCTION

This new book, which builds on and extends my earlier *Working Out of Doors with Young People*, again offers ideas for creative activities, where staff can develop exercises to suit the participants they work with and the varied environments within their reach.

Safety
With the increased public awareness of accidents and issues in the field of Outdoor Activities, all those involved in training need to be even more safety conscious. Each section of this new book has been expanded to provide additional suggestions and guidance for the planning of activities and for safety concerns during the sessions.

I have been fortunate enough to talk over some of the main safety considerations with several key people involved in outdoor work. The points they see as of particular importance have been included in the planning and safety sections of each chapter, together with guidelines from recent safety documents and publications. Some of these points show my own personal concerns which I feel need more emphasis.

How this book will help
The contents of this book represent a selection of successful activities and games developed over many years of working in a variety of outdoor situations. They provide a valuable resource for anyone working, or wanting to work, out of doors with young people. With some optimism I would like to think that those who have not already been bitten by the outdoor bug will be tempted to try out some of these ideas.

Leaders expecting to find a book full of ready made lesson plans will be disappointed, since the pages have been designed to give *basic* ideas for exercises and games. Most staff will need to consider the experience of the young people they are working with, the resources available, and the outdoor conditions.

By careful selection, the ideas contained in the book can be included in a planned programme for:
• residential work
• a training course lasting several weeks
• or a 'one-off' day-trip.
Some attention to the appropriate sequence and variety of activities would be necessary depending on the circumstances.

Most of the activities have been successful with a broad range of young people between the ages of eight and eighteen, consequently it is quite deliberate that specific age groups have not been recommended in each entry. Many of the activities have also been used on a wide range of staff training courses, particularly of the 'Training the Trainer' type.

It will be worth bearing in mind that whilst the order of exercises within a section is interchangeable, the more technically and physically demanding activities generally appear towards the end of the chapters.

The layout and design of the book are intended to give instant visual impact to help inspire young people, hence the emphasis on cartoons. But the notes are mainly aimed at the workers. The book therefore has a dual purpose. Participants should not normally be expected to work through these exercises alone. Some ideas for indoor activities have been included which are intended for the young people to use.

The approach to outdoor work in the book has three main fundamentals, which should be apparent in all of the exercises. These are:

- to ensure that the participants have **fun** in their work
- to allow **all** individuals to be **actively involved** within their capabilities
- and to provide activities that are carefully planned and run to ensure proper **safety standards**.

Be careful out there!

The author and the publisher cannot be held responsible in any way for accidents or injuries which occur in the course of these games and exercises. The leader or teacher with responsibility for the group should ensure that the activities in this book are interpreted in a safe and reasonable way by **all** individuals involved.

Leaders and teachers involved in any outdoor work with young people should be familiar with the book *Safety in Outdoor Education* produced by the Department for Education.

ACKNOWLEDGEMENTS

In all stages of writing this book I have received help and support from numerous sources. I would particularly like to thank the following people:

Steve Brodie - Head of Hagg Farm Environmental Education Centre (Nottinghamshire County Council - Education)

Roy Pike - Resource Coordinator, Outdoor Education Supplies (Nottinghamshire County Council - Education)

Pippa Manson - Head of Environmental Education Support Service (Nottinghamshire County Council - Education)

Hilary Palmer - East Midlands Orienteering Association, Coaching Coordinator

Alan Dearling - Publishing and Production Director, Russell House Publishing Ltd
Alan has made numerous suggestions for improvement both to this book and to its predecessor *Working Out of Doors With Young People*. In addition he wrote substantial sections of the chapter on Other Outdoor Activities.

Geoff Lloyd - Teaching colleague/Outdoor Education

Dave Batty - Teaching colleague/Outdoor Education

Stuart Collins - East Midlands Orienteering Association

Alan Dearling would like to thank Ian Harding, Alan Taylor and especially Dave Kelf for advice on activities in Chapter 9.

I am grateful to everyone else who has contributed their support, guidance and criticism in order to help me complete this book.

PLANNING AND SAFETY

Preparation and Planning

Safety

Choosing Outdoor Centres

Minibuses

Travelling Abroad with Youth Groups

References, Organisations, and Addresses

IN THIS CHAPTER

In this chapter I have attempted to place emphasis on the importance of planning and on safety guidelines. All of us involved in outdoor education must continually strive to ensure safety, so some of the points included in the introductory section of my earlier book, *Working Outdoors with Young People*, have been rewritten or modified, and other important considerations have been added to provide a more comprehensive coverage.

As outdoor work continues to increase in popularity with young people, these suggestions may prove helpful - when used alongside guidelines referred to in this book - in maintaining an enjoyable and safe approach.

These notes are concise and represent personal priorities, but they follow closely many of the concerns expressed in such essential reading as the Department for Education booklet, *Safety in Outdoor Education*. They also cover some of the main concerns of key people involved in outdoor work whose comments and opinions have been invaluable.

The games, exercises and guidelines contained in this book relate mainly to low level environments in summer conditions.

The author and the publisher cannot be held responsible in any way for accidents or injuries which occur in the course of these games and exercises. The leader or worker with responsibility for the group should ensure that the activities are interpreted in a safe and reasonable way by all individuals involved.

More specific guidance on particular activities and pursuits is given in the introductory pages of chapters three to nine.

PREPARATION AND PLANNING

These notes may be useful both for local work and for residential ventures.

Aims and Objectives of the Venture
One of the first tasks when planning any outdoor venture should be to establish clear educational aims - such as providing opportunities for young people to work together in a responsible and constructive way. For multi-activity programmes there could be a range of objectives which may include some of the games and exercises in this book.

Leadership Qualities
With the exception of canoeing, most of the exercises and games in this book could be attempted by staff who are fairly new to this sort of work, providing that their initial ventures are not too ambitious, and that they work well within their level of experience.

Good leadership is of course very important in all aspects of outdoor work. One of the first questions I always ask myself before proceeding with an activity is "Would I be happy for my own children to take part in it?" The 'in loco parentis' responsibilities of leaders when working with young people need careful consideration.

The leader must:

- have relevant experience of the activities to be pursued;
- have undertaken suitable training and achieved recognised qualifications when these are relevant;
- be alert and aware of the safety aspects of the activity;
- maintain good discipline and to check that The Country Code is being followed;
- pre-plan remedial actions for foreseeable emergencies and be able to display sound judgement in difficult circumstances;
- attain an appropriate level of physical fitness. Search and rescue operations or accident situations call for a high level of physical and mental response.

PLANNING AND SAFETY

Teamwork

In any planning, it is of great benefit if the workload is shared between all adult members, and a clear strategy for responsibilities and duties agreed as early as possible. This becomes essential when planning residential ventures. Of course, teamwork also includes the young, and many benefits can be gained by their full involvement during the planning and preparation stages.

Research and Reconnaissance

Residential ventures to outdoor centres and camp sites will require thorough research during the months preceding the expedition. Ordnance Survey maps, guide books, local interest books and publications from National Park Visitor Centres can all provide valuable information and enhance the overall success of the visit.

On many occasions a reconnaissance visit to the area can prove valuable. Study the general layout, the possibilities for training exercises, and the potential dangers and hazards. A thorough look around the camp site or centre in advance will aid the smooth running of operations, and will enable staff to identify safe limits before the venture begins.

Safety Preparations

These key questions are of particular importance and have been included here to give special emphasis at the planning stage. They are addressed in greater depth later in this chapter.

- Will the staff be working within their own experience?
- Have the risks been fully assessed?
- Are the planned activities appropriate for all members of the group?
- Are all leaders sufficiently experienced, trained or qualified?
- Have all staff completed appropriate first aid training?
- Will all staff be fully prepared and briefed?
- Will vehicles be checked for their roadworthy condition?
- Do all staff know the emergency procedures and location of emergency services?

Informing Others and Obtaining Approval

Good communications are essential in the planning stages of any off-site work. The diagram later in this chapter, *Planning and Preparation for a Residential Visit or Camp,* will give some idea of the minimum communication stages advised when planning for a residential outdoor activity venture or camp.

The written consent of parents/guardians is essential, and they should be informed as early as possible about the kind of activities that are contemplated.

The youth organisation or school will have overall responsibility and will need to know full details of the plans at an early date, as will the local authority responsible for outdoor work.

Other colleagues may need to be consulted where plans cut across their routines.

Outside agencies including landowners and specific activity providers may need to be approached for permission or approval.

Briefings

For residential ventures, several briefing sessions will be necessary in the weeks leading up to the departure date. The final briefing session should be taken very seriously and emphasise the purpose of the visit, safety procedures, potential hazards, expectations and standards of behaviour. In particular, strict rules concerning smoking, drinking and sleeping arrangements should be clearly understood. This would be an appropriate time to remind participants about rewards and sanctions. Clothing and equipment will need to be checked before the party gets under way.

Discipline

It is with some regret that I feel the need to add a word of caution. Despite the planning and organisation that goes into outdoor activities, and regardless of how much effort is put in to make the exercises enjoyable, some young people will still be inclined towards activities that they might think of as mischief, but which staff might consider harmful or dangerous to themselves, to other members of the party or to the countryside generally. It is very important that leaders know the young people in their charge, and occasionally exclusion may prove a safer option.

Environmental Concerns

As a point of some importance *The Country Code* may be found on page 29. All outdoor groups need to be particularly conscious of the impact of their activities on the environment and local communities. Staff have a responsibility to educate the young people they work with to be considerate and sensitive towards environmental concerns. With careful thought, activities can be planned with minimal impact, and over-use of sites can be avoided.

Alternative Plans

It is advisable to have some alternative ideas in mind in case the original plans need to be altered. The usual reason for having to abandon activities is bad weather. Many unexpected problems tend to spoil the original plans, and these could be disastrous for the venture unless alternative activities have been planned. For example permission may unexpectedly be withdrawn for using a training area, the minibus may break down, a member of the group may suddenly become ill, or certain activities may become unavailable.

Insurance

Insurance cover is strongly recommended for the majority of work suggested in this book. Leaders will need to check with their authority or organisation about the extent of insurance provision for their activities. Additional cover may be necessary for specific situations excluded in the policy. Parents/Guardians will need to be informed about these arrangements.

Residential Visits and Camps

Planning and preparation can make all the difference. The timetable on the next two pages will help you to address all the points raised here.

6 MONTHS OR EARLIER

- ☐ Check numbers of male and female places available and exact dates.
- ☐ Confirm names of staff and other adults.
- ☐ Request full details of centre's safety policies before booking.
- ☐ First monthly meeting with the group to outline initial plans.
- ☐ Meetings with other colleagues who need to be informed.
- ☐ First monthly planning meeting with staff and adults.
- ☐ Letter to parents with agreed price.
- ☐ Start collection of money and parents' consent slips.
- ☐ Fitness training plan begins.
- ☐ Delegation of tasks and responsibilities.
- ☐ Initial approval/forms completed.
- ☐ Check if any members of the group need financial assistance or other special requirements (e.g. medical, diet, etc.).
- ☐ Appropriate training for staff and adults.
- ☐ Check that all people are fully informed at this stage.

Note: Procedures for booking popular centres may need to be completed much earlier.

4 OR 5 MONTHS

- ☐ Check travel arrangements.
- ☐ Give clothing and equipment list to all participants.
- ☐ Request permission/bookings for various activities: e.g. orienteering, cycle hire, etc.
- ☐ Begin plan of outdoor activities programme in liaison with other staff and adults.
- ☐ Book equipment: e.g. canoes, trailer, tents.
- ☐ Check sizes required for boots, waterproofs, etc.
- ☐ Make contact with additional assistants.
- ☐ Continue preparations with group members, i.e. advice for clothing and equipment, map reading practice.
- ☐ Ensure course leaders are familiar with DFE: *Safety in Outdoor Education*
- ☐ Update information to other colleagues via notice board or other communication.

3 MONTHS

- ☐ Staff team visit venture area and centre for activity planning and safety reconnoitre.
- ☐ Detailed planning for activities including route cards, risk assessments and foul weather alternatives.
- ☐ Indoor or evening activities planned in relation to group size and staffing ratios.
- ☐ First aid training updated.
- ☐ Continue meetings with other staff/assistants involved.
- ☐ Check if additional insurance is needed.
- ☐ Continue preparations with group members: casualty code, safety precautions, use of equipment, e.g. compass.

2 MONTHS

☐ Detailed menu completed?

☐ Option activities and participants decided?

☐ Parents' consent and other approval received?

☐ Full equipment list complete.

☐ Continue preparations with group members, i.e. country code and further map reading or route planning.

☐ Staff training where necessary.

☐ Check all group members for any special medical requirements.

☐ Provisional itinerary to be distributed and displayed.

1 MONTH

☐ Continue preparations with group members, i.e. expectations in terms of effort, involvement, teamwork and targets.

☐ Are staff fully familiar with emergency procedures, where to get help, and Ordnance Survey maps studied.

☐ All approvals received?

☐ Give information booklet to group members and parents, containing aims of the venture, final itinerary, details of centre, equipment list, rules, country code, etc.

☐ Check any special travel arrangements.

☐ Order food list.

☐ All money collected?

1 WEEK

☐ Briefing with all group members. Include clear statement of rules and expectations.

☐ Briefing with staff and other colleagues. Give final detailed plans and recap main points in *Safety in Outdoor Education* and other relevant guidelines.

☐ Check vehicles for roadworthy condition.

☐ Collect and check equipment.

☐ Practice pitching tents and using stoves. This is especially important if camping expeditions are planned.

☐ Deliver advance stores to centre if necessary.

☐ Are all people fully informed of plans?

DAY 1 - BEFORE DEPARTURE

☐ Check vehicles.

☐ Final briefing with all group members. This must include dos and don'ts during the journey.

☐ Check clothing and equipment.

☐ Check weather forecast.

SAFETY

Group Size

All the exercises and games in this book are designed for small groups. A maximum group size of ten participants to one adult worker is strongly recommended in most cases, and where possible, two experienced adults should accompany groups working off-site. With mixed groups, there must be a staff member of each gender.

The staffing ratio will need to be more favourable when working with young people with special educational needs or when conditions are more hazardous.

For initial canoe training, a ratio of 1:8 boats is recommended in the BCU's safety checklist.

First Aid

Staff involved in outdoor work will need to be familiar with first aid techniques, including resuscitation. A minimum training level can be achieved by completing the one day 'Emergency Aid' course of the Red Cross. Consideration should be given to higher qualifications in first aid for staff who are intending to spend a lot of time on off-site ventures. All assistant adult leaders should have an adequate working knowledge of first aid. This is especially important when groups are split up to allow separate activities. First aid kits should be appropriate to the nature of the venture, and careful thought should be given to the best places to keep them, in case they are required in an emergency.

Equipment

The safety of participants depends largely on the generous provision of appropriate protective clothing and equipment to suit the nature of the activities and the outdoor conditions. Detailed lists of equipment are not included, as this information is contained in many of the well known outdoor handbooks, manuals and reference books such as those listed in the relevant chapters of this book. Leaders will need to decide on the suitability and safety of equipment. This includes inspecting items that are frequently in use and likely to become worn, and replacing them as necessary. Equipment checks are strongly recommended at the start of activities to ensure that all participants are equipped in an appropriate way.

Much valuable outdoor work can be done in the local environment however, without the need for expensive equipment and clothing.

Safety Procedures at Outdoor Centres

The following important points have been briefly summarised here as a helpful checklist for visiting leaders. Each note will require a clear explanation from the centre head.

- Always keep in mind the possibility of a fire, and be familiar with the centre's fire procedures.
- A no-smoking rule is a sensible rule at outdoor activity centres.
- Ensure that medical arrangements have been fully understood by members of the group who have expressed a concern.
- Check that all leaders know where first aid equipment is to be found.
- Display the telephone number and address of the nearest doctor.
- Be aware of the route to the hospital.
- Be prepared to record and report accidents and illnesses. The head teacher or head of the youth organisation should be informed of serious accidents or illnesses.
- Carry a list of emergency contact phone numbers.
- Check the centre's procedure for power failure.
- Always obtain a daily weather forecast and be prepared to review the planned activities.
- Establish an efficient system of communication between leaders and centre staff.
- Only drive vehicles within authorised limits.
- Maintain high standards of discipline and behaviour within the group.
- Use regular briefing sessions with the group to emphasise safety concerns.
- Emphasise rules with the group - e.g. no smoking, no alcohol, no entering dormitories of the other gender, no leaving of the centre without permission, etc.
- Protect members of the group from any forms of abuse.
- Ensure that adequate supervision is maintained.
- Explain to participants which areas are out of bounds.
- Be vigilant about food hygiene conditions.

Weather Check

Leaders should be fully aware of how changes in weather conditions could affect their planned activities, especially from a safety point of view. Extreme weather conditions cannot always be forecast in advance, and leaders will often need to show sound judgement in their decisions. Alternative plans, escape routes and cancellation of activities are all essential considerations when leaders have responsibility for the safety of their groups. Weather forecasts are readily available through television, radio, the press and by telephone. National Park Visitor Centres provide especially useful weather information.

Emergency Contacts

All adult members of the group should be aware of and have ready access to emergency contact phone numbers. These are likely to include:

- the Head or Warden of the Outdoor Centre
- the Head of the group's organisation or school
- parents/guardians
- mountain rescue
- police
- doctor

Daytime and evening numbers may be needed.

Accident and Emergency Procedures

The following recommended procedures have been extracted directly from the most up-to-date guidelines available, the Department for Education's *Safety in Outdoor Activity Centres: Draft New Guidance, May 1994*. Only the first section of the emergency procedures is given below. Leaders will need to study this document in full, especially for guidance on more serious incidents.

The recommended procedures are:
- Establish the nature and extent of the emergency.
- Make sure all other members of the party are accounted for and safe.
- If there are injuries, immediately establish their extent, so far as possible, and administer appropriate first aid.
- Establish the name(s) of the injured and call whichever emergency services are required.
- Advise other party staff of the incident and that the emergency procedures are in operation.
- Ensure that an adult from the party accompanies casualties to the hospital.
- Ensure that the remainder of the party are adequately supervised throughout and arrange for their early return to base.
- Arrange for one adult to remain at the incident site to liaise with the emergency services until the incident is over and all children are accounted for.
- Control access to telephones.

CHOOSING OUTDOOR CENTRES

The term 'outdoor centres' in this chapter refers to specialist establishments which provide leadership in outdoor and adventurous activities. These centres will also provide residential facilities for participants. They may be under local authority control or privately managed enterprises.

These notes attempt to identify some important questions which need to be asked before visiting groups make any commitment. They are based on recent guidelines given in the documents noted at the end of this chapter. These questions could be asked by any leader or parent who is naturally concerned about safety provisions for their charges or children.

- Are the staff qualified with the appropriate national governing body?
- Does the centre have a published code of practice for all activities?
- What staff ratios will be used for the planned activities?
- Will the staff follow the guidelines listed in the DFE *Safety Guidelines for Outdoor Education*?
- Are the staff competent to work with the particular age and ability group?
- Does the centre have a code of conduct for visiting groups?
- Can the centre head define clear responsibilities of their staff and visiting groups?
- What alternative options are likely to be available in the event of bad weather or illness?
- Does the provider comply with the relevant health and safety regulations?
- Does the provider complete risk assessments for the activities to be undertaken?
- Does the provider adopt recommendations of the Local Fire Authority?
- Does the centre have substantial public liability insurance cover?
- Is equipment adequately maintained and suited to the activities?
- Are the staff trained for dealing with accidents and emergency situations?
- Do all staff hold relevant qualifications in first aid?
- Are the centre's vehicles and trailers kept in a roadworthy condition?
- Does the provider encourage responsible attitudes to the environment as an integral part of the programme?

Preferably a detailed response to these questions should be available to leaders and parents making enquiries to outdoor centres. This information should be made available to head teachers or other senior officers who have overall responsibility for the authorisation of ventures. The leaders of visiting groups also need to be quite clear about their own responsibilities.

An **accreditation scheme** is currently being developed by the United Kingdom Activity Centre Advisory Committee (A.C.A. C.). Centres with membership of the accreditation scheme will provide an assurance to potential participants that appropriate standards of quality and safety are being met.

If a centre cannot provide reasonable details about provision, then advice should be sought from an experienced representative who is competent to make appropriate enquiries and judgements.

MINIBUSES

The most practical and economic way of getting groups of young people and their kit to places where they can learn and expand their experiences of LIFE.	Noisy, uncomfortable, illegal, frightening contrivances that incompetent leaders can turn into the worst possible thing... - a potential DEATH trap.

Rather melodramatic perhaps....but leaders should regard the minibus with the same concern that they would any other important piece of equipment, and ensure that users are fully briefed, properly trained and completely competent. (Including themselves!)

Best practice and legislation on technical matters, such as seat belts or roof racks, and on personal competence levels will continue to evolve and leaders should try to keep up to date. Guides, such as the *Manual on School Minibuses* referenced at the end of this chapter, cover the matter more fully and are essential reading.

Check-list
A short check-list might include:

Paperwork
- The tax disc, insurance and MOT should be valid for the *whole* period of the trip.
- Correct authorisation to use the minibus must be obtained from the relevant authority.
- All drivers' qualifications must be verified:
        - no endorsements on licence;
        - driver over 21;
        - driver has authorisation card (in the case of local authority trips);
        - full licence - of course!
- Is the vehicle covered by membership of one of the major motoring associations?
- Does the minibus contain the relevant, up-to-date maps?

The Mechanicals
- At least two weeks before the trip:
        - check the minibus service history and serviceability and act to rectify defects;
        - for longer journeys, make sure that the minibus is equipped with forward-facing seats;
        - ensure that seat belts, seat fixings, etc. conform to current regulations and practice: seek professional help if unsure.
- Immediately before departure do all the things that we often don't do. Check that:
        - oil level and tyre pressures are correct;
        - all the lights work;
        - radiator and windscreen wash bottles are topped up.

The Drivers

- Where are the access doors and how are they operated?
- How many people are you allowed to carry? Does one adult equal two children?
- What are the safe limits for loading the roof rack?
- Where are the first aid kit and fire extinguisher?
- How many hours are you allowed to drive? Driving when over-tired can kill.
- What do you do in the event of breakdown or accident?

The Journey

- Ensure that equipment is stowed tidily - not in the gangway!
- A second adult aboard can help reduce driver distractions and maintain discipline and interest.
- Make constructive use of travelling time with quizzes, observation games and following route maps. You can find useful ideas in *The New Youth Games Book* by Alan Dearling and Howie Armstrong (Russell House Publishing).

TRAVELLING ABROAD WITH YOUTH GROUPS

The Department for Education's *Safety in Outdoor Education* booklet outlines the following points for leaders planning visits abroad:
- advantages of using reputable tour operators;
- medical requirements for particular countries;
- members of party to carry address and telephone number of hotel/hostel;
- emergency contacts to be submitted to the authority in advance.

Individual local authorities have produced detailed guidelines for taking minibuses abroad.

Many of the issues covered earlier in this chapter on 'Planning and Safety' are worth looking at again in the context of taking youth groups to other countries. Basically, the further you travel away from base, the more important planning and preparation become. There are also additional complications which can arise because of different laws, language, currency, cultures and traditions and the vagaries of travel.

A worst possible scenario might be: *The mini-bus breaks down, you are not in one of the motoring organisations and have to pay for repairs and a tow; you arrive at the port late and the ferry cannot accommodate the bus on the next crossing. You travel through France and get stopped by the police, and you realise that you don't have adequate insurance cover, haven't modified the headlights to be angled for driving on the right and don't have the GB sticker on the rear of the vehicle. Then, you reach the 'idyllic' camp site in the south of France and find it to be smelly, with poor sanitation and facilities, and situated between the local superstore and a garage on the main trunk road! From then on, the holiday really takes off. One party member becomes ill with severe stomach pains and is rushed to hospital. On the same day, three of the group get caught shop-lifting in a small local store: the police suggest that the children should be taken back to the UK. Then the mini-bus breaks down again....................................Need I say more?*

Unfortunately, I and my colleagues have experienced all of the above and worse on trips. There are some fairly simple preparations which can make the task of planning and managing a trip abroad more effective and help it to be fun and safe.

Planning, Equipment and Finances
- Make sure that at least one member of staff has visited the proposed accommodation and the area(s) to be visited. Evaluate the potential problems with accommodation and try to sort them out in advance. Is access to the accommodation when the group arrive straightforward? Obtain details of what facilities and activities exist, and make contact/bookings where necessary.
- Prepare a draft 'programme' of activities and trips and organise any pre-booking that is necessary.
- Equipment needs: buying extra equipment which you may already possess back home is costly and unnecessary - so make sure that needs have been evaluated both for the party as a whole and for individuals. This may include anything from crockery and food, through sleeping bags, waterproof clothing, walking and climbing boots, right up to canoes and mountaineering ropes.
- Make sure that someone has calculated how much money will be required to cover all the expected expenditure and emergencies. Remember 'extras' such as road tolls.
- Make sure that insurance for leaders and group members is adequate.

Travel
- Find out well in advance what requirements there are for:
    - vehicles and driving in the countries you will pass through, and obtain maps and other reference materials;
    - travel by boat, train, aircraft;
    - passports, visas and currency.
- Check that everyone has a valid passport. It is useful to ask all participants to record their passport number and its expiry date on the application form. Some children may not have British passports and it is as well to prime everyone that they may need to go through a different channel at passport control and to arrange supervision of this.

Health
- Check that health matters have been thought through. For instance:
    - Do any of the party have special health requirements/medication/or special diets?
    - What happens if someone gets ill or injured?
    - Have all the party had the required vaccinations and immunisation for the countries you are visiting?
    - Find out the address/telephone number of the nearest doctor/hospital to where you are staying.

People
- Staffing levels need to be higher to cover for emergencies, illness, pressures of driving etc. Have all the staff arranged to be available for the dates of the trip? Does the group need:
    - Specialist activity skills/qualifications?
    - A particular balance of male/female staff?
    - Members who can speak particular languages?
- Hold briefing/planning meetings with all the group members so that they know what to expect and what is expected of them. Keep parents informed and ensure that permissions have been obtained in writing. Make sure that there is a contact phone number for every member of the party just in case of emergencies.
- It is most important to agree about rules and 'boundaries' in advance:
    - Does the accommodation have its own rules and regulations?
    - What are the agreements on swearing, smoking, drinking?
    - What cultural rules are there in the areas you are visiting, such as clothing?
- Have games and diversions, such as travel games or packs of cards, to keep everyone entertained and involved. Journeys can be long and tedious!

Cultural Issues
- Plan menus in advance, perhaps making use of local foods. Some young people can be fussy about food. If possible try to arrange 'taste ins' of dishes special to the area to be visited prior to the trip.
- At a preparation meeting you may wish to cover:
    - How to greet people.
    - The geography, history and customs of the area.
    - How to travel around. Do you need a carnet for the Metro? Is it normal to queue? And so on.
    - 'Faux pas' to be avoided in verbal and body language.
    - Other cultural or religious matters: where and what beachwear is permitted, or what is suitable clothing and headgear for visiting religious buildings.

- If you are visiting a country where participants cannot speak the language it is useful if they learn a few simple phrases before the trip. Also, in case they need to seek assistance, they might carry a badge or card with the base telephone number plus a few relevant phrases in the local language.

Most of the suggestions are common-sense, but the more complex trips abroad, such as adventure safaris do require additional detailed planning and preparation if they are to be safe and successful. They will also probably require more local knowledge and expertise than is required for similar activities within the UK. Don't be put off. It is encouraging that more and more international and European trips are being organised for young people and their educational value is immense.

The British Council may be a source of additional information.

Other options to consider include:

- **Exchange trips** and specially organised cultural visits may be worth considering and can provide help with funding. Many schools and educational establishments already have links which can be extended. The Youth Exchange Centre at The Central Bureau, Seymour Mews House, Seymour Mews, London W1H 9PE is funded by the Government to provide a range of services which encourage educational trips abroad. They administer the grants for youth groups and are the national agency for the Youth in Europe programme.

- **Use of specialist travel and activity companies.** There are literally thousands of organisations which you can 'buy into'. These offer anything from cycling and canal holidays through to organised camps and activity 'packages'. You can find details of many of these organisations in directories in the library, such as the 'Education Year Book' (Longman).

REFERENCES

These references may be useful both for local work and for residential ventures.

Safety in Outdoor Education, Dept. for Education, HMSO, 1989
This includes a detailed list of publications and addresses.
Guidelines for Offsite Educational Visits and Activities in the UK, Nottinghamshire County Council - Education, 1993
Safety in Outdoor Activity Centres: Draft New Guideline, Dept. for Education, 1994
Manual of Guidance on School Minibuses (Draft), Nottinghamshire County Council, 1994
An Introduction to Basic Minibus Driving and **Essential Minibus Driving**, Tony Dring, ROSPA, The Priory, Queensway, Birmingham, W. Midlands B4 6BS
Minibus Safety, Community and Youth Workers Union, 202a The Argent Centre, 60 Frederick Street, Hockley, Birmingham B1 3HS
Important News for Drivers of Minibuses, Minimum Test Vehicles and Towing Trailers, Dept. of Transport, DVLA, Swansea
Safety on School Journeys, NUT, Hamilton House, Mabledon Place, London WC1H 9BD
Your Minibus - is it Legal?, Community Transport Association, High Bank, Halton Street, Hyde, Cheshire SK14 2NY
Outdoor Adventure Activity Providers - Code of Practice, UK Activity Centre Advisory Committee, 1994
Hagg Farm Environmental Education Centre - Safety Codes of Practice, Nottinghamshire County Council - Education, 1994
Visits and Activities Guidance Notes, Nottinghamshire County Council Leisure Services - Youth and Community
Safety Practices in Adventure Programming, Priest and Dixon, available from Adventure Education, Penrith

USEFUL ORGANISATIONS AND ADDRESSES

Mountainwalking Leader Training Board
Crawford House, Precinct centre, Booth St. East, Manchester, M13 9RZ
Sports Council
16 Upper Woburn Place, London WC1H 0QP
British Red Cross Society
9 Grosvenor Crescent, London SW1X 7EJ
St Andrew's Ambulance Association
48 Milton St., Glasgow G4 0HR
St John Ambulance
1 Grosvenor Crescent, London SW1X 7EF
Basic Expedition Training Award
Central Council of Physical Recreation, Francis House, Francis St., London SW1P 1DE
British Canoe Union
Adbolton, West Bridgford, Nottingham NG2 5AS
Royal Yachting Association
RYA House, Romsey Road, Eastleigh, Hampshire SO5 4YA
HM Coastguard
Dept of Transport, Room 8/1, Surley House, High Holborn, London WC1V 6LP

Duke of Edinburgh Award
Gulliver House, Madeira Walk, Windsor, Berks SL4 1EU
Girl Guide Association
17/19 Buckingham Palace Road, London, SW1W 0PT
Scout Association
Baden-Powell House, Queen's Gate, London SW7 5JS

OUTDOOR WORK AND THE NATIONAL CURRICULUM

Physical Education in the National Curriculum

Geography in the National Curriculum

IN THIS CHAPTER

This chapter identifies aspects of outdoor work within the physical education and geography programmes of study of the National Curriculum for England and Wales. Although many leaders and instructors may not be involved with the implementation of the National Curriculum in schools, there is much in these proposals that is a direct result of good practice, and is consequently worthwhile or desirable for young people wherever they may be.

This chapter relates to the National Curriculum Draft Proposals, published in May 1994, and takes account of the changes and modifications requested by teachers over recent years. Extracts from the Draft Proposals in this chapter are shown in italics.

This is a personal response to the Draft Proposals and includes interpretations which may or may not be representative of other groups of people.

Outdoor work in its variety of activities is firmly established in the National Curriculum for physical education and geography, and is seen as an essential aspect of the overall education of young people.

My earlier book, *Working out of Doors with Young People*, was published in 1987 and preceded the National Curriculum by several years; indeed many of these activities were developing during the 1970s and 1980s. It is therefore satisfying to see that much of this work can be matched to the current National Curriculum proposals, and is seen as desirable pursuits in a broad educational framework. Although there is no intention to systematically match up every page with National Curriculum requirements, I have chosen several examples where activities seem to be particularly appropriate.

PHYSICAL EDUCATION IN THE NATIONAL CURRICULUM

The general programme of study for physical education across the primary and secondary school age range includes many familiar aspects where outdoor work can make a great contribution. For example the references to *promote healthy lifestyles* through the *development of cardiovascular health, flexibility, muscular strength and endurance* brings to mind the demanding nature of walking, orienteering and canoeing, to mention just a few activities. *Positive attitudes* are important in outdoor work, and *coping with success and failure* will occupy time at the conclusion of activities. Team exercises such as SEARCH AND RESCUE (page 45) or assessment tasks such as STRETCHERS (page 42) are likely to generate these reactions due to the complexity and level of involvement necessary.

Young people can be *taught to be mindful of others* through situation exercises like HYPOTHERMIA (page 40), where numerous useful procedures are followed in the caring for a patient.

To ensure safe practice, students must be taught *to respond to instructions and signals within established routines*. The NIGHT NAVIGATION exercise (page 43) provides several opportunities for these responses, set in a realistic situation.

Students will soon become aware of the need for *particular clothing, footwear and protection* as they participate for example in the exercises in the CANOE ACTIVITIES chapter. Life will become very uncomfortable, or worse, if due consideration is not given to this advice.

CARRY SEATS (page 106) requires some preparation work on *how to lift, carry and place equipment safely*. Even with four people involved, the total weight of the passenger and other bits and pieces amounts to quite a strain for most individuals.

An important point contained in the General Programme of Study is the need for *teachers to select material to enable individual pupils to progress and demonstrate achievement*. This applies to all ability levels and to various forms of disability which teachers and group leaders may need to cater for. *Appropriate provision should be made* for these young people if possible.

Programme of Study for Pupils Aged 8 to 11 - (Key Stage 2)

At this stage, pupils are required to pursue outdoor and adventurous activities as one of six areas of activity. A range of *different environments* are recommended including *school grounds and premises, parks, woodland or seashore*. Numerous adventurous exercises are offered in this book, though care should be taken over the level of difficulty for pupils in this age range. Basic orienteering courses close to the school or in local parks, such as the POINTS COURSE (page 55), STREET ORIENTEERING (page 53), or THE SWEET CHASE (page 66) can provide a feel of adventure for many pupils who may not have experienced such opportunities. Contrasting environments will of course be available to schools that can offer youth hostelling or camping expeditions.

Pupils should be taught challenges of a problem-solving nature, using suitable equipment, which include planning, recording and evaluating whilst working in small groups. Hopefully the chapter on PROBLEM SOLVING will provide some ideas which may be adapted for the needs of the individual schools. OBSTACLE RELAY (page 95), MODEL CARGO BOATS (page 103) and SIGN POST (page 107) are particularly recommended for pupils in this age range, providing numerous challenges and scope for decision making.

Programme of Study for Pupils Aged 12 to 14 - (Key Stage 3)

There is some choice at this stage, with outdoor and adventurous activities making up one of the six units. Work on the school site is still possible, although some schools may have access to a variety of activities within reasonable travelling distance. The chapter on CANOE ACTIVITIES for example contains lots of ideas for young beginners' groups. *The techniques and skills specific to* canoeing may be practised in games such as BEGINNERS' SLALOM (page 145) and SKILLS RELAY (page 146) ultimately leading to the British Canoe Union's tests and certificates. *Pupils following the full unit should be taught at least one other outdoor and adventurous activity to include, where possible, offsite work in unfamiliar environments.* Schools that are able to offer another adventurous activity could make use of Chapter Three: FINDING THE WAY, where appropriate sessions provide a solid foundation for pupils who would like to continue their ventures in a competent and responsible way at a later stage.

LEADING IN TURN (page 32) meets the National Curriculum requirements particularly well as it provides the opportunity for *pupils to be taught a variety of roles, including leading and being led.*

Programme of Study for Pupils Aged 15 to 16 - (Key Stage 4)
Again, some choice of activities will be offered for students in this age range. Outdoor and adventurous activities are one of six areas, and the chosen aspects are to be pursued at some depth.

STRETCHERS (page 42) would be appropriate for older students who are being taught *to plan, prepare and undertake a journey safely, encompassing one or more activity(ies) in an unfamiliar environment.* The ROUTE PLANNING preparation exercise (page 30) provides a simplified introduction, though more detailed plans may need to be made depending on the ability or experience of the group. Careful thought would of course be necessary in choosing the area in which to work.

Students should be encouraged *to develop their own ideas by creating challenges for others.* Many students respond well to these opportunities, finding the challenge rewarding and enjoyable. PUZZLE TRAILS (page 115) shows a variety of ways of creating head-scratching problems while following a route around a village. Ideally, the most persevering students would plan and set up the complete activity, but some groups may need more guidance to achieve success with this time-consuming task. In the ORIENTEERING chapter more challenges can be set with STRIP MAPS (page 57). Here the students work in pairs to map a small area and set out a small orienteering course for another pair to follow.

As would be expected, students of this age should have developed their ability to cope with *more complex techniques and safety procedures appropriate to the activity(ies) undertaken.* TEAM RESCUE (page 147) is an example illustrating how more competent students can work together to undertake a very demanding deep water manoeuvre.

Although MENU PLANNING (page 74) may give a very light-hearted impression, the undertones are intended to be more serious. The careful planning of a menu for a three day camp provides opportunities for the students to learn about *the effects of nutrition on the body* especially in relation to outdoor activities. The multi-problem HYPOTHERMIA exercise (page 40) may be referred to again, as it clearly demonstrates *the effects of nutrition and climatic conditions on the body.* An alternative simulation could be planned for a group to deal with a casualty suffering from heat exhaustion.

The final section of the Draft Proposals for physical education gives a list of *statements which describe the types and range of performance which most pupils should characteristically demonstrate by the end of a key stage.* These statements will be valuable for teachers who are responsible for assessing the progress of their children, but will also have a wider value for other leaders and instructors who need to plan suitable activities for their groups.

GEOGRAPHY IN THE
NATIONAL CURRICULUM

The Draft Proposals for geography are encouraging for teachers who are particularly interested in outdoor work, as there is much emphasis on fieldwork throughout the document.

Programme of Study for Pupils Aged 6 to 7 - (Key Stage 1)

Geographical enquiries are recommended for children in this age range, with much of their learning *based on direct experience, practical activities and fieldwork in the locality of the school.* In particular, pupils will be involved in an investigation of the *quality of the environment in a locality*, and *about changes in that environment.* I have personally not tried out the exercises in this book with children as young as this, but the ENVIRONMENTAL QUALITY SURVEY (page 117) may provide some ideas for structuring their work.

Programme of Study for Pupils Aged 8 to 11 - (Key Stage 2)

Geographical skills in their fieldwork enquiries will involve the use of simple instruments. The weather theme could make use of thermometer, anemometer and wind vane as shown in the WEATHER exercise (page 38). In the locality of the school a compass can be used to help identify geographical features. A simplified version of the OBSERVATION GAME (page 122) could be useful here, giving practice at setting compass bearings on real features or landmarks.

STREAM SURVEY (page 126) gives a well tested approach to finding evidence through fieldwork that streams *erode, transport and deposit materials.* With careful choice of location for this team exercise pupils can learn much *about landscape features associated with rivers.*

For the *Environment* theme, it should not be too difficult to find an example of a major development such as a new road or a new shopping centre that is being planned or is under construction. A field-visit to such a site would help pupils to establish *that human activities affect the environment.* LAND FOR DEVELOPMENT (page 128) is about an investigation into a new mine site, but could be adapted for most types of development. By studying the developers' plans, pupils will find *ways in which people manage their environments*, and how the impact of development may be reduced.

Programme of Study for Pupils Aged 12 to 14 - (Key Stage 3)

Mapwork skills are particularly important at this level, and many of these skills including *use of scale to measure distances, following routes, identifying relief and landscape features and using maps in decision-making exercises* can be developed through orienteering or map and compass walks. The ORIENTEERING and FINDING THE WAY chapters contain many basic ideas that would be useful for this work. BEGINNERS' TRAINING MAPS (page 52) gives some advice on producing suitable, uncomplicated maps (mainly for the local area). Contact with a local orienteering club is worth consideration, and advice or help with the mapping of school grounds could prove to be invaluable.

At Key Stage 3 there is a choice between rivers and coasts for the investigation of geomorphological processes. Depending on the school's locality, either theme may be studied at first hand through fieldwork enquiries. FLOOD RISK (page 127) suggests methods of calculating a stream's velocity and discharge, using simple measuring techniques. This data collected from primary sources may help in the understanding of *the causes and effects of river floods and how people respond to flood hazard.*

The draft proposals include the study of an ecosystem. Pupils are required to learn how vegetation is related to climate, soil and human activity. One clear-cut method of investigating these relationships is to make recordings at points along a route from a valley floor, up a suitable slope, to the high land above the valley. This method is often known as making a transect. SLOPE STUDY (page 125) shows in a simplified way how ecosystems can change as height is gained.

Settlement studies for pupils in this age group involve investigations of urban land-use patterns, services and layout design. Particular emphasis is placed on *the impact of change on different groups of people.* VILLAGE SURVEY (page 114) provide fieldwork ideas relevant to this theme.

Environment issues are investigated in the final theme at Key Stage 3. Pupils will need to understand *why some areas are viewed as being of great scenic attraction, how conflicting demands on the areas can arise, and about the issues which result.* Through their studies pupils will also understand *how some leisure activities can affect areas of environmental value.* CONFLICT (page 119) goes some way towards addressing these issues and may be set in the context of a National Park.

Programme of Study for Pupils Aged 15 to 16 - (Key Stage 4)

Fieldwork remains an important part of the geography curriculum for students in this age range, with the GCSE examination boards being responsible for syllabus designs and assessment procedures. Enquiry methods and investigations through fieldwork experiences are generally accepted as essential components of all GCSE geography courses.

REFERENCES

Physical Education in the National Curriculum, Draft Proposals, May 1994, Ref: COM/94/058
Geography in the National Curriculum, Draft Proposals, May 1994, Ref: COM/94/054
Both booklets are produced by School Curriculum and Assessment Authority and the Central Office of Information, Newcombe House, 45 Notting Hill Gate, London W11 3JB, Chairman: Sir Ron Dearing, CB.
Outdoor and Environmental Education in the National Curriculum, available from Adventure Education, Penrith

FINDING THE WAY

ARE WE THERE YET ?

In This Chapter

All of the exercises in this chapter are intended to combine map navigation with some planned activity during the walk.

Even when working with complete beginners, everyone in the group should be given some responsibility for navigating a small section of the walk, with the leader at hand to give advice and instruction. As map and compass skills are developed, the group may be given more demanding navigation routes to tackle, with or without the leader at hand, depending on the nature of the terrain, weather conditions, group equipment, and the level of responsibility of the group.

Most of the exercises have been chosen for their 'fun' value, but they would also contribute towards character building; participants who have successfully completed a demanding adventure programme are likely to be more aware, more prepared, and more confident.

This chapter offers a few ideas which may be used in short local walks, which may well be in parkland or in quite easy country near to the edge of town. The same ideas could also be used with groups working in moorland, hills or mountains, depending on the leaders' experience and qualifications.

The skills and experience needed to lead groups in these different environments vary considerably. It is therefore very important that staff are familiar with the distinctions between these areas, and plan activities within their own experience and training. The effect of adverse weather conditions also needs to be considered.

Three types of environment have been given below to help leaders identify appropriate levels of difficulty:

LEVEL 1: Lowland Countryside - at any time of year.
LEVEL 2: Moorland, Hills and Mountains - in anything other than winter conditions.
LEVEL 3: Moorland, Hills and Mountains - in winter conditions.

Environment Descriptions

Level 1: Lowland Countryside

These areas normally have well defined paths or tracks and easily identifiable features. They tend to be close to public services such as roads and telephones, and rural communities are nearby. Although no specialist qualification is necessary for working with groups in these environments, the leader should have sufficient personal experience of walking in similar areas, and should preferably arrange a preparatory visit in advance of the groupwork, or at least research the specific area.

Level 2: Moorland, Hills and Mountains (in anything other than winter conditions)

These environments include open moorland, hill and mountain areas, such as those found in the Peak District, Dartmoor, North Wales and the lower fells of the Lake District. Staff planning walking activities in these environments will need to be fully competent in navigational skills and must have considerable hill walking experience. Recommended training and qualifications are noted later in this section.

As this book is mainly targeted towards basic, introductory outdoor work, no description of Level 3 is needed here.

Planning and Safety

Some important considerations have been outlined in Chapter One. These recommended guidelines apply to one-off walks in lowland countryside and to walks in moorland, hills and mountains, which may be part of a residential outdoor activities programme.

In addition to the points in Chapter One, the following notes are worth remembering:
- Check frequently that the group is keeping together, and that no-one is left trailing behind.
- Look out for individual problems, such as blisters, exhaustion, etc. Small problems can soon develop into bigger ones, which could easily affect the success of an activity.
- Leave details of the group and route with a responsible person, and inform them of the group's return.
- Respect rights of access and be sensitive to the way of life in rural areas.

It will be apparent that most of the activities here will require a considerable amount of preparation time, plus continuous communication and encouragement throughout the sessions, if they are to be successful.

Recommended Training and Qualifications

Local Education Authorities, Youth Services and outdoor centres organise courses for staff wishing to lead groups in lowland countryside and in moorland and hill environments.

The basic *Expeditionary Training Award* is administered by the Central Council of Physical Recreation and provides training for those wishing to lead others in 'normal country' environments.

The *Summer Mountain Leader Award* is organised by the Mountain Leader Training Boards of the United Kingdom. The scheme of training and assessment is appropriate for staff aiming to lead groups in moorlands, hills and mountains (in anything other than winter conditions).

The *Mountaineering Instructors Award (MIA)* is also appropriate for countryside, moorland, hill and mountain environments (in anything other than winter conditions).

Higher level qualifications include the *Mountain Leader Winter Award*, organised by the Scottish Mountain Leader Training Board.

The main reference used in compiling this information was: *Countryside, Moorland, Hillwalking and Mountain Leader Guidelines,* Nottinghamshire County Council - Education, 1993.

Publications

Safety in Outdoor Education, Dept. for Education, HMSO, 1989
Mountaincraft and Leadership, Eric Langmuir, Scottish Sports Council, ISBN: 0-903908-75-1, 1984
First Aid Manual, St John Ambulance, St Andrew's Ambulance Association and the British Red Cross Society, Dorling Kindersley, 1987
Mountaineering, Alan Blackshaw, Penguin, 1990
British Mountaineering Council - Mountain Code, British Mountaineering Council, 1988
Land Navigation: Route Finding with Map and Compass, Wally Keay, Duke of Edinburgh's Award, 1989
Mountain Navigation, Peter Cliff, ISBN:0-904405-48-6, 1986
Safety on Mountains, Barry, J. and Jepson, T., British Mountaineering Council, 1987
John Merrill Walk Guides: catalogue available from Trail Crest Publications Ltd, Milne House, Speedwell Mill, Miller's Green, Wirksworth, Derbyshire DE4 4BL

Organisations and Addresses

Basic Expedition Training Award, Central Council of Physical Recreation, Francis House, Francis Street, London SW1P 1DE
British Mountaineering Council and Mountainwalking Leader Training Board, Crawford House, Precinct Centre, Booth Street East, Manchester M13 9RZ
Scottish Mountain Leader Training Board, Caledonia House, 1 Redheughs Rigg, South Gyle, Edinburgh EH12 9DQ
Youth Hostels Association, Trevelyan House, 8 St Stephens Hill, St Albans, Herts AL1 2DV
Scottish Youth Hostels Association, 7 Glebe Street, Stirling FK8 2JA
Ordnance Survey, Romsey Road, Maybush, Southampton SO9 4DH

THE COUNTRY CODE

The importance of The Country Code cannot be over-emphasised. The leader has responsibility for teaching the rules of The Country Code at an early stage in outdoor work. Some of the rules may need to be stressed several times during the course of a day or at the start of each session. A natural way to start the group thinking about The Country Code is at a rest stop.

ROUTE PLANNING

Route planning should be an important part of any training programme for walking activities. The hypothetical exercise on the next page attempts to simplify the awesome task of completing a full, detailed route card.

The format given may be used as a basic outline for use with a variety of maps and routes. The group leader will need to fill in alternative answers, as shown in the example route card. The students are then required to cross out the wrong answers by studying each leg of the route, as shown on an overlay. The overlay may be tracing paper or transparent film. These can be duplicated so that several people can complete the exercise together.

Equipment
Ordnance Survey maps
set of route cards
   (with 2 alternative answers
   completed each time)
overlays
   (with points circled and numbered,
   and route marked)
compasses
pencils
paper or string to measure distances

Value
Specific map and compass skills, including:
- reading six figure grid references
- identifying map symbols
- measuring distance
- using a scale
- estimating heights
- estimating time
- setting grid bearings
- converting to magnetic bearings
- identifying suitable escape routes

Hypothetical Exercise

The standard format for the route card is shown in CAPITAL LETTERS.
Alternative answers have been written in small letters and underlined.

START by giving the six figure grid reference for POINT 2.

ROUTE CARD No.3

POINT 1 (GRID REFERENCE <u>123456</u>) TO POINT 2(_____)

POINT 1 AT THE START OF THE ROUTE IS A <u>car park</u> OR <s>camp site</s>?

THE DISTANCE BETWEEN POINTS 1 & 2 IS ½km OR <u>1km</u>?

THEN continue by crossing out the WRONG answer each time as shown.

POINT 2 (GRID REFERENCE _____) TO POINT 3 (_____)

POINT 2 IS AT A <u>path junction</u> OR <u>bridge</u>?

THE DISTANCE BETWEEN POINTS 2 & 3 IS <u>1km</u> OR 1½km?

THE ROUTE BETWEEN POINTS 2 & 3 <u>follows a stream</u> OR <u>climbs a slope</u>?

POINT 3 (GRID REFERENCE _____) TO POINT 4 (_____)

POINT 3 IS AT A <u>stream junction</u> OR <u>hill summit</u>?

THE DISTANCE BETWEEN POINTS 3 & 4 IS <u>2km</u> OR 1km?

THE MAGNETIC BEARING BETWEEN POINTS 3 & 4 IS <u>90°</u> OR <u>180°</u>?

THE ROUTE BETWEEN POINTS 3 & 4 <u>follows a ridge</u> OR <u>crosses a road</u>?

POINT 4 (GRID REFERENCE _____) TO POINT 5 (_____)

POINT 4 IS AT A <u>small lake</u> OR <u>small wood</u>?

THE DISTANCE BETWEEN POINTS 4 & 5 IS <u>2½km</u> OR 1½km?

THE MAGNETIC BEARING BETWEEN POINTS 4 & 5 IS <u>270°</u> OR <u>200°</u>?

THE ROUTE BETWEEN POINTS 4 & 5 <u>follows a rocky edge</u> OR <u>goes downhill</u>?

THE HEIGHT AT POINT 4 IS <u>300 metres</u> OR <u>200 metres</u>?

POINT 5 (GRID REFERENCE _____) TO POINT 6 (_____)

POINT 5 IS AT A <u>stream junction</u> OR <u>road junction</u>?

THE DISTANCE BETWEEN POINT 5 AND POINT 6 IS <u>1km</u> OR 1½km?

THE MAGNETIC BEARING BETWEEN POINTS 5 & 6 IS <u>15°</u> OR <u>50°</u>?

THE ROUTE BETWEEN POINTS 5 AND 6 <u>crosses a brook</u> OR <u>climbs a slope</u>?

THE HEIGHT AT POINT 5 IS <u>50 metres</u> OR <u>100 metres</u>?

THE TOTAL DISTANCE OF THE ROUTE IS <u>8km</u> OR 6½ km?

THE TIME TAKEN TO WALK (AT A PACE OF 4KM PER HOUR) IS <u>4 hours</u> OR <u>2 hours</u>?
(NOTE: TIME SHOULD BE ADDED TO THIS FOR CLIMBING HILLS AND RESTS)

A SAFE ESCAPE ROUTE FROM POINT 4 WOULD BE TO <u>follow the stream path in a northerly direction to the road</u> OR <u>climb down the steep slope to the south</u>?

LEADING IN TURN

Although the idea for this exercise is borrowed from mountain leadership training procedures, the navigation and leadership experience can be equally valuable for younger groups.

Procedure
At the start of the walk, the adult leader would brief the group on leadership responsibilities. This would include:
- keeping the group together;
- following the rules of The Country Code;
- checking equipment and clothing; and
- accurate navigation.

Depending on the aims of the venture, it is recommended that all individuals in the group are given adequate practice in map reading and setting a compass bearing from the map.

Suggested Map and Compass Routine at the Start of Each Leg
To save time at the start, have the maps ready folded and inserted into map cases.

A. Reading the Map
1. Put your finger on the map in the place you are standing at now.
2. Put another finger on the map in the place you intend to walk to.
3. Study the map to decide the best route to take.
4. Set your map so that it is lined up with the landscape ahead of you.

B. Setting a Compass Bearing from the Map

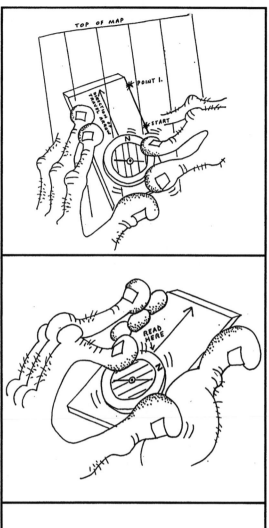

Step 1: Lay your compass on the map so that the long edge touches the point where you are standing (START) and the point where you intend to walk to (POINT 1). Make sure that the direction of travel arrow on the compass plate is pointing in the direction you intend to go on the map. <u>Then</u>, keeping the compass base plate pressed firmly on the map, turn the compass housing so that the lines inside your compass line up with the North/South grid lines on your map, and the N points to the top of your map.

Step 2: Pick up the compass and read the bearing. Turn the compass housing anticlockwise to add 5½°. (This is necessary because of the difference between magnetic north and grid north. The figure is accurate for 1995 and decreases by about ½° over 3 years.)

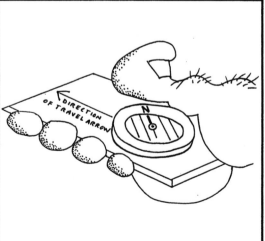

Step 3: Holding the compass flat, move your whole body around until the red magnetic needle lines up with the N on your compass housing. The direction of travel arrow on your compass plate should now point towards the place you intend to walk to.

C. Estimating Distance

There are several quick ways of estimating the distance you have to walk:

- Use the edge of your compass (which is usually marked in centimetres).

> On a 1:25,000 map: 1cm = 250 metres
> On a 1:50,000 map: 1cm = 500 metres

- Use your thumb or finger width to estimate distance. (Test this on the map scale.)
- Use the grid squares to give a quick visual guide to distance.

> One grid square on an Ordnance Survey map = 1 kilometre

D. Estimating Time

An approximate estimate of the time you expect to take to walk each leg of the route can be very helpful. With practice this routine becomes more accurate. *Naismith's Rule* can be used as a rough guide:

> 5km per hour + 30 minutes per 300 metres climb + time for rest stops

Hence a 1km leg with 100 metres of climb should take about:

Walking 1km:	12 minutes
Climbing 100m:	+ 10 minutes
Rest stop	+ 5 minutes
TOTAL	27 minutes

This formula will need to be adjusted for conditions underfoot, weather and fitness of participants.

During the Walk

During the walk the adult leader would give each individual, or pair, responsibility for navigating and leading the group for a given leg of the route. All members of the group should be encouraged to navigate throughout the walk, even though it may not be their turn to lead.

The idea can be used in all kinds of terrain, depending on the ability or experience of the group, i.e. parkland, woodland areas with many paths and tracks, moorland areas with few paths, etc.

Value

- leadership experience
- map and compass navigation skills
- communication
- group responsibility
- self confidence
- decision making.

COLLECT AND RECORD

Procedure

1. Give each team a list of 15 items to find along the route, a map of the route, and a record card to complete along the way. Each team will also need a plastic bag or jar with ventilation holes in the top, in which to keep the specimens.

2. Make sure that all students can identify the 15 items, and stress the importance of collecting live (undamaged) specimens. See sample list below.

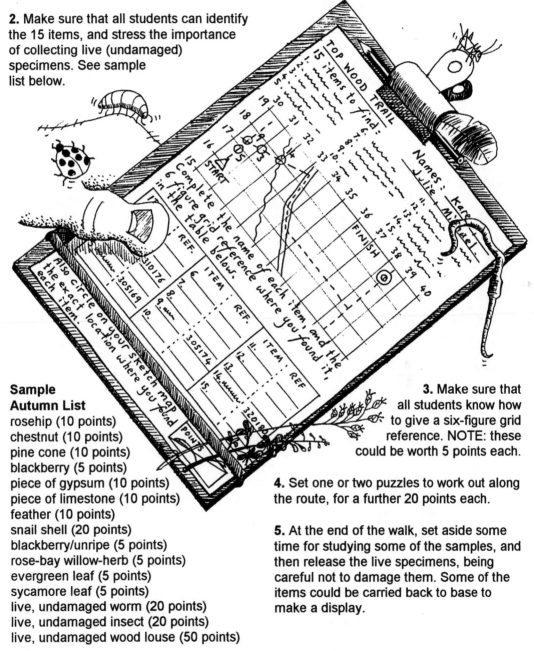

Sample Autumn List

rosehip (10 points)
chestnut (10 points)
pine cone (10 points)
blackberry (5 points)
piece of gypsum (10 points)
piece of limestone (10 points)
feather (10 points)
snail shell (20 points)
blackberry/unripe (5 points)
rose-bay willow-herb (5 points)
evergreen leaf (5 points)
sycamore leaf (5 points)
live, undamaged worm (20 points)
live, undamaged insect (20 points)
live, undamaged wood louse (50 points)

3. Make sure that all students know how to give a six-figure grid reference. NOTE: these could be worth 5 points each.

4. Set one or two puzzles to work out along the route, for a further 20 points each.

5. At the end of the walk, set aside some time for studying some of the samples, and then release the live specimens, being careful not to damage them. Some of the items could be carried back to base to make a display.

NOTE: Special care should be taken not to include rare fauna and flora in the list.

MEMORY GAMES

This is a useful exercise to throw in at a rest stop during the exercise. The leader divides the group into two teams. The first team is instructed to lay down a jacket, and place 15 items on it. The items may be selected from pockets, rucksacks, and from the immediate area. The second team is then given 30 seconds to memorise the 15 items. After they have been covered up, the second team must attempt to write down as many of the items as possible in 2 minutes. After the list has been checked, the teams change over, and team 1 attempts to achieve a higher score.

Map Memory
Another memory exercise can be done as the group walks along. The leader asks one member of the group to look at the map, and memorise 5 features which the group will pass, along his or her leg of the route. These features must then be identified (without further reference to the map). The next member of the group then chooses another 5 features, and so on.

EQUIPMENT DECISIONS

This training exercise may be completed indoors or in the area close to base. The aim of the exercise is to provide opportunities for decision making and handling equipment. The exercise may take about 30 minutes to prepare, and about one hour to complete; but it should be worth the effort. A maximum of 10 people is recommended, plus 2 leaders.

Procedure

1. Before the group arrive, lay out all the equipment and waterproofs needed for a summer hill walk. Bags or containers with labels may be used as substitute items if necessary.

2. Divide the group into teams of 4 or 5. Ask two people from each team to collect all the items for their team. Alternatively, treat this as a survival exercise and allow each team to choose the 10 most important items out of approximately 20, and then prioritise them on a list.

3. The leader then announces that the group are about to start their imaginary walk. The weather is dry and sunny and they must pack their rucksacks, but first they must decide, as a team, exactly where each item will be placed.

4. When both teams are ready, the whole group may start to walk around a set route. At a suitable point, the leader would stop the group and instruct them to put on their waterproofs, as a heavy rainstorm has suddenly started. Those people who had already put on their waterproofs or who had packed them at the bottom of their rucksacks would be given 10 penalty points. Others receive 10 bonus points.

5. The group then continues along the walk. At the next point, the leader stops the group and asks them to set a compass bearing from their map. Those who had their map and compass inside their rucksack would be given 10 penalty points. Those who were ready would receive 10 bonus points.

6. The group then continues along the walk. At the next point, the teams could go through the routine of making an imaginary brew of tea, using small stoves and other items from their rucksacks, which would then be repacked. At this point, the leader, having observed both teams, could give out more penalty points and bonus points for tidiness and rucksack packing.

7. The group continues along the walk again. At another point, the leader would inform the group that one person from each team has suddenly become seriously ill, and two people from each team must prepare to walk 10 miles across the hills to telephone for a doctor. Each team must decide exactly which items will stay with the casualty and friend, and which items will be packed when the two people go off for help. After the rucksacks have been packed, the leader may discuss this final problem, and give out more penalty points and bonus points.

8. Finally, all items would be checked back in, important points recapped, and team totals worked out.

WEATHER

All outdoor groups should be encouraged to develop an interest in weather forecasting, as their activities may need to be modified as a result of the daily forecast. This practical session at the base is intended to give young people first hand experience of collecting various kinds of weather information.

Listen to a pre-recorded tape, (or video?), of the general forecast for the following day; e.g. Radio 4, 5-55 p.m., and make notes under specific headings.

Make specific notes from the daily weather map, and find out the meaning of the figures and symbols on a station circle.

Phone the weather station for your region, and make specific notes.

Record the outdoor shade temperature in degrees celcius, using a dry bulb thermometer.

Record the cloudiness outside in oktas - e.g. 2 oktas or ¼ cloud cover.

Identify the type of clouds visible.

Record wind direction using an improvised wind vane, (made by the students?).

Record wind speed using an improvised anemometer and Beaufort Scale.

Depressions - Find out the sort of weather associated with depressions.

Air Pressure - If a barometer is available, record air pressure and note any change in pressure?

Further work - Find out how temperature, wind, cloud and rain change in hilly areas.

At the end of the session ask for volunteers to use their recordings to plan and present a T.V. style weather forecast for the day.

WINDY DAY

A windy day can present good opportunities for testing qualities of resourcefulness, perseverance and co-operation. The aim of this exercise is to test the effectiveness of the wind shield by boiling a kettle of water out in the open.

Procedure

1. At the base, the group is divided into two teams, and given the materials to design and construct a type of wind shield which will offer protection on three sides:

> strong polythene
> string
> tape
> scissors
> bamboo canes

The stove, with kettle in position, may be set up so that dimensions can be estimated. Tape and string may be used to attach the polythene to the canes. The final product should be collapsible, so that it can be carried in or on a rucksack to the test site.

2. All the necessary items for making a mug of tea should be packed, and a suitable navigation walk planned.

3. While some members of the group are setting up the wind shields and lighting the stoves, another team could use a large sheet of polythene and cord to improvise another larger wind shield to shelter the group.

NOTE: Special care should be taken in strong winds to avoid fire spreading to the wind shield and vegetation. This exercise may not be appropriate in very dry conditions.

HYPOTHERMIA

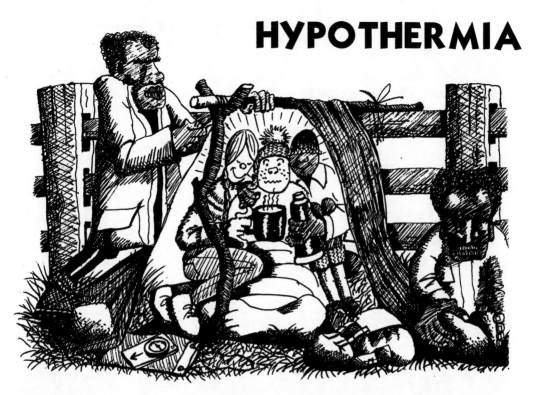

Procedure: A little instant acting is required for the success of this multi-problem exercise. At the start of the walk the leader could brief the group on the causes of hypothermia, and the signs, symptoms and treatment. This information is best shown on a laminated card. (Refer to first aid books or mountaineering books.) The group could then be informed that at some stage during the hike one member of the group would start to show the obvious signs of suffering from hypothermia. The leader would discretely choose one individual to act as the hypothermia casualty. The other members of the group would be expected to respond in a responsible manner and work quickly as a team to make the casualty warm, and to improvise a shelter. The group would also be required to complete an accident message card which would involve the use of an Ordnance Survey map to note the exact location, and to work out a suitable route for some members of the group to go for a doctor.

Equipment needed for each group
laminated information and instruction card
lengths of cord
large polythene sheet for improvised shelter
survival bag
hot drink in flask or stove, and kettle, etc.
Ordnance Survey map
map case
compass
pencil
accident message card with spaces to fill in
additional clothing and equipment
   (depending on weather conditions and terrain)

Value
initiative
caring for others
problem solving
instant acting
communication
outdoor survival
safety awareness
teamwork
map reading
thoroughness.

WHAT'S WRONG?

What should be the correct way ?

STRETCHERS

At a pre-planned point during the walk, a card may be given to the group, with instructions explaining how to cope with a suspected fractured leg. This group initiative exercise would also involve the construction of an improvised stretcher, preferably using items that have been carried, or dropped off in advance.

The group would also be required to write out an accident message card, which would involve the use of an Ordnance Survey map to note the exact location, and to plan a suitable escape route.

After the padded splint has been strapped to the patient (See first aid books for the correct method!) and the stretcher has been checked by the leader, the group may then plan a simple obstacle course to test the ability of the group to carry the stretcher and patient safely. One penalty point could be given for each fault on the obstacle course. The obstacle course should not be too hazardous, or the stretcher patient may need real treatment! The stretcher should only be carried at a walking pace, taking care to keep the patient horizontal at all times.

Equipment

laminated instruction card
2x 6 foot poles and 2x 4 foot poles
lengths of lashing cord
strong plastic sheet or survival bag
    (for stretcher mattress)
Ordnance Survey map
compass
map case
accident message card with spaces to fill in
pencil
splints
improvised padding and wrapping

Value

teamwork
initiative
caring for others
problem solving
fun
communication
outdoor survival
safety awareness
perseverance
NOTE: this exercise is especially suitable as an assessment task, using some of the above criteria.

NIGHT NAVIGATION

Courses planned on public paths and bridleways in fairly easy country can present an attractive challenge at night. The following procedure list was given to all members of my group at an essential training meeting before a night navigation exercise. NOTE: It may be necessary to inform the local police and farmers or land owners of your plans.

Safety Points

This is a very demanding exercise for participants and for staff involved. The following considerations may be helpful:

- Are the participants mature enough to complete this exercise?
- Are all the participants trained in map and compass navigation?
- Are <u>all</u> participants reliable when unsupervised?
- Are there any known hazards in the area?
- Are there sufficient members of staff or other adults who are willing to help, and will they be fully briefed?
- Are you fully prepared for emergencies?

Procedure

1. Before you start, check that you have all the necessary items, including:

> map
> control card
> compass
> watch
> whistle
> torch
> spare batteries
> waterproofs

2. Before you start, write your names on the control card, and fill in your time out, final return time, and emergency phone number.

3. You will be timed out in pairs. You must keep together throughout the course. Your control card will NOT be signed at the checkpoint cars unless you are together.

4. You must keep to the route shown on the map. The route is on public paths and minor roads. Do not attempt to cut across any farmland or woods, as these are private!

5. Be sensible. Remember, we will need to use this area again in the future!

> Keep as quiet as possible - especially near farms and houses.
> Close all gates.
> Do not drop any litter.
> Do not flash your torch around too much.

6. The main aim is to complete the course by checking in at each of the three checkpoint cars in order.

7. Do not be too hasty.

> Be absolutely certain of your position on the map at all times.
> Double check your intended direction of travel at each point.
> Hold your map so that it is pointing in the direction you want to travel.

8. Do not follow other pairs without checking your own map. They may be lost!

9. If you are completely lost:

> Weigh up the situation calmly.
> If you still feel unsure about moving on, retrace your steps to a known point.
> Do not split up.

10. If you have wandered completely out of the area, you are completely lost and you are over the final return time:

> Find a telephone and phone the emergency number shown on your control card (or the police).
> Do not split up.

11. If you become ill or have an accident:

> Make your way to the nearest checkpoint car if you are capable.
> If you cannot do this...
>> Keep as warm as possible.
>> Call for help.
>> Flash torches until help arrives.
>> Do not split up.

12. You must report to the finish and hand in you control card, map, compass, etc., even if you do not complete the course.

ENJOY YOURSELF, BUT BEWARE OF THE MONSTER!

TEA

SEARCH AND RESCUE

This multi-problem exercise always seems to be appealing to young people. The exercise tends to be most exciting at night, in unfamiliar country, although successful search and rescue exercises can easily be planned in daytime in a park or on paths near the edge of town.

This is a very demanding exercise at night. Refer to SAFETY POINTS in the NIGHT NAVIGATION exercise.

Procedure
A card is given to the group with a message, such as:

> *"Injured and exhausted person located at grid reference 211359*
> *(wall corner). Make padded splint for sprained or fractured*
> *ankle, keep patient warm and comfortable, and help back to*
> *base by most suitable route."*

The group should be given full responsibility for organising the search party with necessary clothing and equipment, navigating accurately, caring for the patient (which may involve constructing an improvised stretcher) and returning to base as a group. Two or three groups could be involved in similar exercises at the same time, each navigating to different points.

One memorable night in Derbyshire, when I was acting as the injured person out on the hillside, making realistic moaning and groaning noises, the group had become so involved in the exercise that one girl broke down in tears when their torches finally shone on my prostrate form.

Value:
group responsibility
teamwork
caring for others
initiative
resourcefulness
communication
navigation
perseverance

ORIENTEERING

I'M LOST!

MAP

In This Chapter

Orienteering has grown in popularity with young people over recent years, and clubs have worked hard to create opportunities for school groups and other organisations. Special events for schools (and groups such as scouts and guides) have become familiar fixtures in the orienteering calendar and some clubs have helped to map school grounds. Recent publications, including those listed later in this chapter, provide a valuable resource for staff introducing orienteering to young people. The National Curriculum recognises the importance of orienteering as an adventurous activity. The 'thought sport', as it is often named, makes a major contribution to the development of healthy young people.

In this chapter I have attempted to provide a sample of training exercises and ideas for beginners' groups. The exercises have been specially designed for groups with limited opportunity for travelling to interesting orienteering areas. If a group is restricted to an urban base, then several indoor and outdoor exercises are still possible. Indoor sessions could make use of orienteering maps with courses marked on them. These are especially valuable for route choice practice, and symbol recognition. There are also many possibilities for indoor orienteering games. Examples in this chapter include: EGG-BOX COURSE, ROUTE CHOICE and O-CARDS.

Map reading in the urban area near the base can also be very successful with groups. STREET ORIENTEERING, as explained in this chapter, may give some ideas for working out courses.

If the group can travel to a nearby park, or open area with public paths and bridleways, then possibilities become more interesting. Exercises designed for such areas include: STRIP MAPS, MEASURE IT COURSE, POINTS COURSE and WINDOW SCORE EXERCISE.

The group may be fortunate enough in having a leader who will take them to an event, organised by their local orienteering cub.

Getting Started

For group leaders who are thinking about orienteering as a possible new activity, may I suggest three initial steps:

1. Try out a few events yourself, join your local orienteering club and make contacts with other club members who may offer help or advice.
2. Read some of the well-known orienteering books such as those listed later in this chapter.
3. Attend a suitable training course as recommended in the following section on training and qualifications.

Important Points

1. A Balanced Programme: The exercises and ideas contained in this chapter are intended to be used along with other more familiar orienteering training exercises, to make up a balanced, comprehensive orienteering course. The leader will need to plan their programme, depending on the needs of the particular group and the resources available.

2. Preparation: As with other activities in this book, orienteering with groups requires a large time commitment form the leader. Thorough planning and preparation are essential for successful orienteering at any level.

3. Access: Most of the training exercises outlined here may be done near the base, or on local public paths or parks, where permission may not be required. If group leaders are planning more ambitious events, in private woodlands or other orienteering areas, then written permission from the landowners is *essential*. Your local orienteering club will be able to give advice on suitable areas to use. Any thoughtless action involving trespass could result in the loss of valuable areas for thousands of orienteers.

4. Supervision: The very nature of orienteering requires the individual to navigate alone, with map and compass, through the countryside. This statement may be true for experienced orienteers, but for many young beginners' groups I would suggest a more controlled approach at first.

Initially the leader could walk around a simple course with the group, showing them how to read and hold the map, and how to conduct themselves out of doors. This controlled stage is valuable for keeping an eye on progress and behaviour.

The leader's method could be changed in the next session by accompanying the group around the first half of the course, and then timing them out in pairs for the second half of the course.

If satisfactory progress is made after a few training sessions, then suitable courses could be attempted, with the participants navigating in pairs or alone. Even when the students are given maximum freedom for orienteering, the leader should always be fairly close at hand, to give help and supervision when necessary.

5. Code of Conduct: The importance of the The Country Code should be stressed with all groups. This is particularly necessary for young orienteers who will be given the responsibility for finding their way around the countryside without close supervision.

6. Success: An important point worth remembering when introducing people to orienteering is the fact that they need not be athletes to be successful. Unlike cross-country running, the orienteer is alone in the forest competing against himself or herself. For many orienteers the feeling of achievement in navigating successfully around a course is sufficient reward for their efforts.

DON'T BE PUT OFF! ORIENTEERING CAN BE GREAT FUN.

Planning and Safety

Much of the general advice given in Chapter One applies to orienteering. The following additional points are more specifically concerned with orienteering, especially at an introductory level.

- Plan *quality* courses rather than *quantity*. i.e. not too long.
- Keep courses simple for beginners.
- Recognise different levels of difficulty imposed by different environments.
- Keep within your own safe limits of experience and training.
- Plan courses suitable for the age or ability of the participants.
- Ensure that you are fit enough to move quickly around the area.
- If possible, choose areas with safe boundaries and few hazards.
- Inform participants of any hazards and tape these off if necessary.
- Beware of areas where risk of abuse could be a problem from strangers.
- Know the location of telephone and emergency routes.
- Always give a clear briefing before the participants begin.
- Check for suitable equipment and clothing (e.g. full body cover).
- Carry a first aid kit and preferably attend a first aid course for orienteers.
- Check for individual medical conditions, e.g. asthma.
- Remind participants to beware of sharp branches which could damage their eyes.
- Where possible, work with small groups, i.e. one experienced leader to ten participants, with additional help if possible.
- Arrange for a more generous staffing ratio when working with younger children, beginners or participants with special needs.
- It is advisable to set a final return time for all participants.
- Stress the importance of checking in at the finish even if they do not complete the course.

Recommended Training and Qualifications

The British Orienteering Federation (BOF) identifies four types of environment which are related to training and qualifications.

A. Schools/Centres and their grounds or other private safe areas
Some background knowledge and experience is recommended for leaders at this level, together with involvement in a short (possibly in-service) course designed for teachers/centre instructors.

B. Local park, permanent course or attending a BOF event
Recommended qualification is the BOF *Orienteering Instructor Award*. Leaders should give participants advice on relocation strategies in preparation for orienteering in these areas.

C. Country Parks and some forests (with clear boundaries)
Recommended qualification is the BOF *Club Coach Award*. A staffing ratio of 1:10 with at least 2 competent staff is advisable at this level.

D. Other areas (including complex or exposed locations)
To be avoided unless weather conditions are favourable and staffing expertise is present. Recommended qualification is BOF *Regional Coach Award* or a *Club Coach with a BOF Grade 2 Controller*.

Publications, Organisations and Adresses

Safety in Outdoor Education, Dept. for Education, HMSO, 1989
Orienteering Guidelines (leaflet), Nottinghamshire County Council - Education, 1993

Available from **The British Orienteering Federation** at Riversdale, Dale Road North, Darley Dale, Matlock, DE4 2HX:

> **Safety Guidelines for Schools, Outdoor Centres and Squads,** British Orienteering Federation, 1994. This leaflet is the main resource for the planning and safety section in this chapter.
> **Mapmaking for Orienteers**, Robin Harvey
> **The British Orienteering Federation Catalogue** of orienteering publications and products.
> **Compass Sport Magazine** - incorporating **The Orienteer** is the official (bimonthly) magazine of The British Orienteering Federation. Subscriptions are available from 25 The Hermitage, Eliot Hill, London SE13 7EH

Available from **Harveys**, who are suppliers of orienteering teaching resources and equipment, mapmakers and publishers, at: 12-16 Main Street, Doune, FK16 6BJ, Scotland:

> **Harvey Map Services Catalogue**
> **Teaching Orienteering: A Handbook for Teachers, Instructors and Coaches**, Carol McNeill, Jean Ramsden and Tom Renfrew, 1987, ISBN 1-85137-020-X. Published in co-operation with The British Orienteering Federation.
> **Orienteering in the National Curriculum - Key Stages 1 & 2: A Practical Guide**, Carol McNeill, Jim Maitland and Peter Palmer, ISBN 1-85137-015-6. Published in co-operation with The British Orienteering Federation.
> **Orienteering in the National Curriculum - Key Stages 3 & 4: A Practical Guide**, Carol McNeill, Jim Maitland and Peter Palmer, ISBN 1-85137-010-2. Published in co-operation with The British Orienteering Federation.
> **Starting Orienteering**, a series of books for school teachers, Carol McNeill and Tom Renfrew.
> **Trail Orienteering**, a handbook on orienteering as an activity for the disabled, Anne Braggins, ISBN 1-85137-090-0
> **Maps!, More Maps!, Using Maps!**, three computer programs that teach children about basic map literacy, for Macintosh computers.

The Forest, a computer game simulating orienteering, available for all BBC computers (Micro, Masters, etc.), Cunning Running Software

BEGINNERS' TRAINING MAPS

The two maps on this page are intended to show how simple it is to produce basic training maps suitable for young beginners. These black and white maps show only the essential information needed for youngsters to find their way on paths and tracks around a suitable safe area with public access. Participants may progress onto courses using the detailed colour orienteering maps by arrangement with local orienteering clubs. Note especially that contour lines have been completely omitted from these beginners' maps, and alternative symbols and labels used to show hills and slopes.

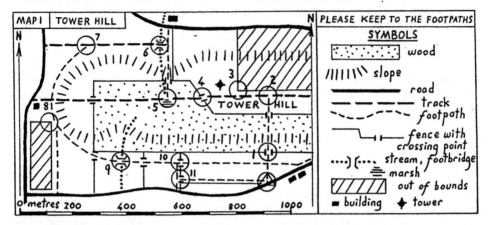

A similar map to the one above can be produced by first making a simplified tracing from a 1:10,000 Ordnance Survey map, and then checking and modifying details in the field. The completed tracing is then photocopied, and the course pre-marked on the maps in red biro. The participants will also need a control description list with spaces for the codes to be written in at each control.

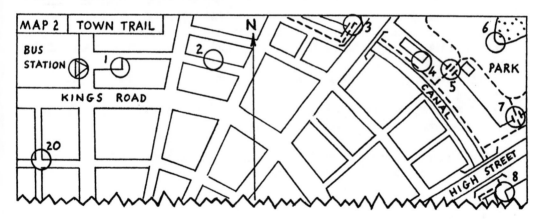

Map 2 shows part of a simple street orienteering map. Notice how most of the street names have been removed to encourage map reading techniques.

IMPORTANT: Map makers must follow the copyright guidelines when Ordnance Survey and other maps are used. For more detailed advice on mapmaking, refer to Robin Harvey's book *Mapmaking for Orienteers* obtainable from the British Orienteering Federation.

STREET ORIENTEERING

POINT ① The steps.
How many steps ?

198, 199

Here are some examples of the sort of question that could be asked on a street orienteering course.
Each question could be given a points value, and the aim is to gain as many points as possible.

POINT ② Church spire
What feature is at the top of the spire ?

GRRR!

POINT ③ Hall entrance
What stone animal is found at this point ?

POINT ④ Hotel hanging sign
How many people are painted on the hanging sign ?

POINT ⑤ Market square (centre)
Sketch the design set into the pavement.

POINT ⑥ Archway
What building can you see through the archway ?

POINT ⑦ Corner building
In what year was this building built ?

1844

TRAVELLER'S REST

BILL'S BAKERY
FAST DELIVERY SERVICE

Many towns and villages produce large scale street maps (often at little or no cost) showing tourist information, bus routes, or conservation areas, etc. These may be ideal for street orienteering, although they will need to be pre-marked and sealed in plastic bags, so they may be used again.

An alternative approach for street orienteering is shown on the next page.

An alternative approach for street orienteering.

An alternative structure for street routes can be on an INSTRUCTION SHEET. Although this method does not involve map reading, it does require participants to follow clear instructions, which may include map symbols.

EXAMPLE :

from the [P] walk north along Victoria Street to the ✝ and turn left at the junction. Pass the [i] on your left and continue for 500 metres to the T. Take a right turn here, following the pedestrian _ _ _ _ _ _ _ under a -}||{-_ to the △.

To prevent people from making disastrous errors it is advisable to include some definite place names at appropriate stages on the instruction sheet, together with a list of map symbols. Extra staff or helpers may be used at strategic points. To give an added flavour to this exercise try writing the instructions in rhymes.

POINTS COURSE

An important feature of any course designed for beginners should be that it allows everyone to experience the feeling of achievement. An obvious way of providing for this is to see that the control flags or markers are located mainly on the paths and tracks (line features), and not hidden away in the middle of the forest.

Another way of designing an orienteering course for beginners is to give each control a set number of points, depending on the degree of difficulty, or the distance away from the start. The beginners then aim to gain as many points as possible, within a time limit, and all is not lost if some of the controls have not been found.

Pairs or individuals are timed out at intervals and timed in, but their overall time is not as important as points on this particular type of course.

The job of checking progress along the course is much easier if the course is planned so that competitors visit the controls in a given order, as shown below, in the completed exercise.

NORTH COMMON POINTS COURSE		NAME(S): Jenny Green and Linda Smith	
TIME OUT : 11-00 a.m.	FINAL RETURN TIME : 1-00 p.m. (YOU MUST RETURN BY THIS TIME !)		
CONTROL ORDER	DESCRIPTION	CODE LETTER	POINTS
1	path junction	Y ✓	5
2	path / track junction	A ✓	10
3	stile (crossing point!)	Z ✓	15
4	footbridge	H ✓	15

NOTE
1. The students will need a training map (similar to Map 1 on page 52) with the course premarked in red biro.
2. This is basically a normal cross country orienteering course with an additional points bonus for each control.

WALK A WORD

The idea of this game is to set out the capital letters of an unknown word, on the ground, by following instructions - giving directions (or compass bearings) and paces. A long piece of string is laid out in the shape of each letter (or chalk may be used on hard surfaces).

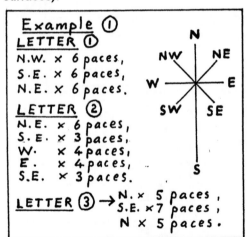

Example ①

LETTER ①
N.W. × 6 paces,
S.E. × 6 paces,
N.E. × 6 paces.

LETTER ②
N.E. × 6 paces,
S.E. × 3 paces,
W. × 4 paces,
E. × 4 paces,
S.E. × 3 paces.

LETTER ③ → N. × 5 paces,
S.E. × 7 paces,
N × 5 paces.

NOTE: Always start facing north. All letters start on an imaginary base line. Some lines return along the same path, to make the string continuous for each letter, e.g.

Letter E = E

Some method of keeping the string in position may be needed, e.g. pegs or sticks.

Each pair could be given a card with instructions for only one word, to reduce the chance of forward planning. Each new word becomes progressively more difficult, i.e. using different letters, longer words, longer paces, and compass bearings.

Example ② (with compass bearings)	LETTER ②	LETTER ③	LETTER ④
LETTER ①	90° × 4 paces,	45° × 6 paces,	0° × 5 paces,
30° × 5 paces,	270° × 4 paces,	125° × 3 paces,	270° × 2 paces,
150° × 5 paces,	0° × 2½ paces,	270° × 3 paces,	90° × 4 paces.
30° × 5 paces,	90° × 4 paces,	90° × 3 paces,	
150° × 5 paces.	270° × 4 paces,	125° × 3 paces.	
	0° × 2½ paces,		
	90° × 4 paces.		

CREATIVE OUTDOOR WORK

STRIP MAPS

Stage One

Each pair is given a small section or strip of map to complete as they walk along a path or track. Accuracy is not essential for this exercise. The idea is to observe the features on either side of the path or track, and mark these on to the strip map. A simplified list of black and white orienteering symbols will be needed.

NOTE: The leader will need to prepare several different outline strip maps with only paths and tracks marked on.

Stage Three

Back at the start maps are checked and then exchanged with another pair. Each pair should now have a new strip map with symbols drawn on, and a simple 3 or 4 point orienteering course marked on to the map. The markers are to be found and collected, using the map drawn by another pair.

Stage Two

Each pair should also set out 3 or 4 red and white orienteering markers on suitable features next to the path. These points should be circled and numbered on the strip map. The markers should be clearly visible from the path.

NOTE: It may be necessary for the students to make up some symbols if they find any useful features which are not shown on their symbol sheet.

NOTE: A simple pacing exercise would be useful in preparation for this activity. As the strip maps will be surveyed at walking pace, the students could count how many double walking paces it takes them to cover a measured distance of one hundred metres.

ROUTE CHOICE

The board for this game, which is intended for two players, is on the next page.

Each player, in turn, carefully marks a route around the course on a copy of the page. Each player moves one square at a time, and records the points for each square in the grid at the bottom of the page. The aim is to achieve the lowest total score for the full course. The numbers in the squares represent the degree of difficulty of the terrain. Two routes may go through the same square, and routes may cross over, but they must not go through the intersection points of the squares.

Finally, compare your routes with those of other people in the group. This page may be reproduced, so that several pairs can play the game.

This is the board for the ROUTE CHOICE game.

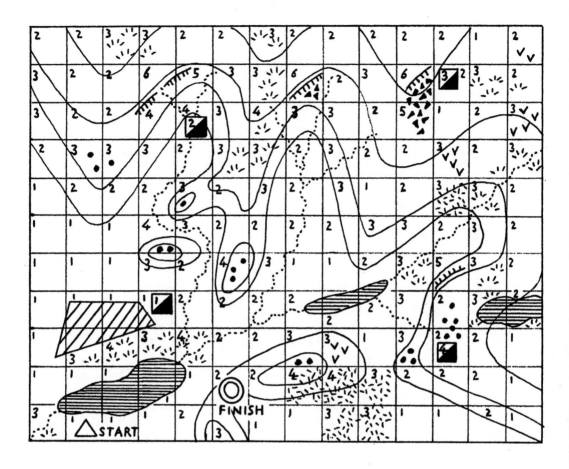

ORIENTEERS ARE?

Which words do you think apply to top class orienteers?
Complete a questionnaire to see what other people think in your group.

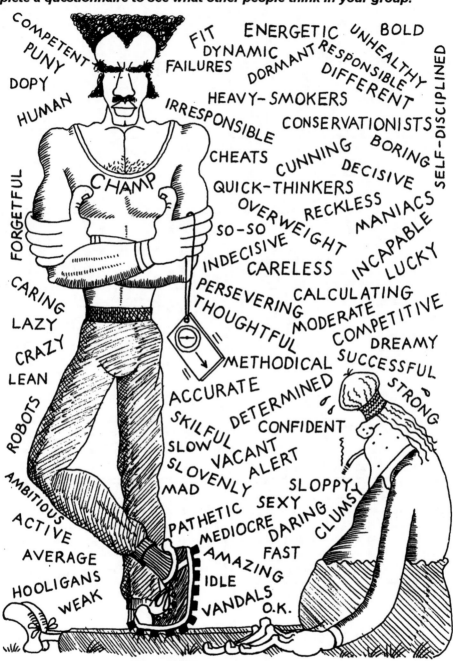

Which words would you like to describe yourself?

O-CARDS

This card game is intended to remind the players of some of the more important orienteering skills, and common errors made, during a competition. First of all a set of 30 normal size playing cards needs to be made. One side of each card is shaded red and white to represent a typical orienteering control flag, and the other side is printed, as shown below.

THE 16 PENALTY CARDS (Minutes are added on for these cards.)

RUSHED! PENALTY +10 minutes	POOR MAP READING. PENALTY +5 minutes	POOR CONCENT-RATION. PENALTY +5 minutes	FOLLOWED SOMEONE TO WRONG CONTROL. PENALTY +5 minutes	TIRED ON CLIMBS. PENALTY +10 minutes	FOLLOWED SIMILAR PATH (PARALLEL ERROR). PENALTY +10 min.	DIDN'T READ CONTOURS. PENALTY +10 minutes	DIDN'T TAKE COMPASS BEARING. PENALTY +15 min.
INJURY. PENALTY +20 minutes	DIDN'T READ CONTROL DESCRIP-TION. PENALTY +5 min.	TOO CAREFUL. PENALTY +5 minutes	TURNED COMPASS 180° OUT. PENALTY +15 minutes	MAP DAMAGED. PENALTY +10 minutes	SYMBOL MISREAD. PENALTY +5 minutes	WANDERED AROUND SEARCHING AIMLESSLY (LOST!) PENALTY +30 min.	NO DETERM-INATION. PENALTY +20 minutes

THE 8 BONUS CARDS (Minutes are subtracted for these cards.)

GOOD ROUTE CHOICE. BONUS −20 minutes	ACCURATE COMPASS BEARING. BONUS −15 minutes	'AIMED-OFF' PURPOSELY TO ONE SIDE. BONUS −10 min.	OBVIOUS FEATURE (ATTACK-POINT) USED. BONUS −10 min.	ACCURATE PACE COUNTING. BONUS −15 minutes	'HANDRAIL' FEATURE USED, e.g. wall, path or stream. BONUS −10 min.	CONSTANT SPEED MAIN-TAINED. BONUS −30 min.	NO TIME LOST AT CONTROLS BONUS −10 minutes

(Also 6 BLANK CARDS are needed.)

The instructions and score card for O-cards are on the next page.

Instructions for O-Cards Game

The cards are shuffled, and laid out at random on a table. The cards are scattered around a start triangle card. the red and white sides face upwards. This arrangement could represent a 'score' course, with the control flags set out around the start. Each player, in turn, picks up any card, reads out the comment, and then places the card on his or her pile. If a penalty card of say 15 minutes is picked up, then a marker is moved along the score card (see below) to add on 15 minutes. Both players start at 100 minutes. If a bonus card of say 10 minutes is picked up, then a marker is moved backwards to subtract 10 minutes. This player then has an extra go, after a bonus card has been picked up. The winnner will have the shortest time, after all cards have been picked up.

THE SCORE CARD
(Each player needs a small marker to move backwards or forwards.)

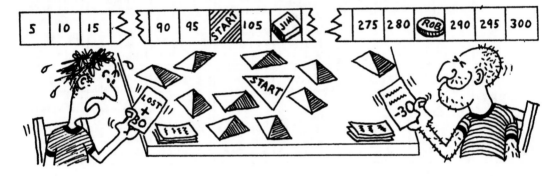

EGG BOX COURSES

This practical exercise requires students first to create their own relief map, using egg boxes, and then to plan their own orienteering course and route. Each pair will need a large sheet of paper or card for the base, egg boxes or egg tray, scissors, pens (blue, black, red) and paper for writing out the control descriptions.

Procedure
1. Examples of simple relief features and landforms are shown using the cut-up egg boxes, e.g. valley, pass, ridge, spur, corrie, knoll, peak, etc.
2. Cut up the egg boxes and lay out the shapes when you are satisfied with their positions.
3. With a blue pen, mark:

3 rivers with 4 bridges

3 lakes   3 marshes

4. Plan an orienteering course with 10 to 15 control points, plus start and finish, and mark these in red biro. (See examples of orienteering courses before you start. There should be some route choice problems for each leg of the course.)
5. With your red biro make a dashed line to show the best route around the course. With your black biro make a dashed line to show an alternative route.
6. Make a list of control descriptions for your course, e.g. 1 = spur, 2 = N. side of lake, 3 = pass, etc. (Refer to your list of terms and sample descriptions.)
7. Finally, volunteers talk their way around their course (to the rest of the group) giving a description of the route and reasons for the routes chosen.

Further Activity
Draw the contour lines around each of the shapes.

PROBLEM CHECK-LIST

	course 1.	course 2.	course 3.	course 4.
Name of area				
Date				
Course distance in km				
Time				
Position				

Look again at each leg of your orienteering course on your map. Shade one small box to show each time you had a problem.

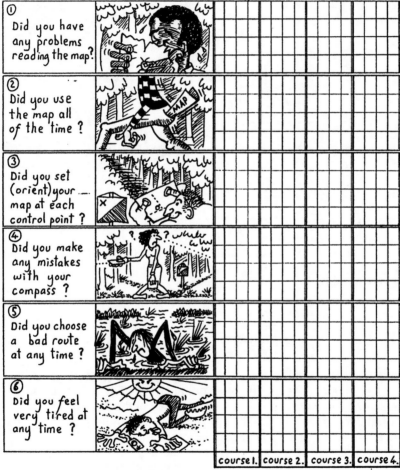

① Did you have any problems reading the map?

② Did you use the map all of the time?

③ Did you set (orient) your map at each control point?

④ Did you make any mistakes with your compass?

⑤ Did you choose a bad route at any time?

⑥ Did you feel very tired at any time?

course 1. | course 2. | course 3. | course 4.

Look again at your completed checklist. What do you think are the three most important ways to improve it?

NOTE: This page may be reproduced to use as a record sheet.

MEASURE IT COURSE

Each pair will need a piece of string 1 metre long, which is marked every 10cm. Instead of looking for the normal red and white orienteering flags, a measurement is made with the string at the points marked on the map. This style of course has the obvious advantage that flags or markers need not be set out beforehand. The participants will need a training map (similar to Map 1 on page 52) with the course pre-marked.

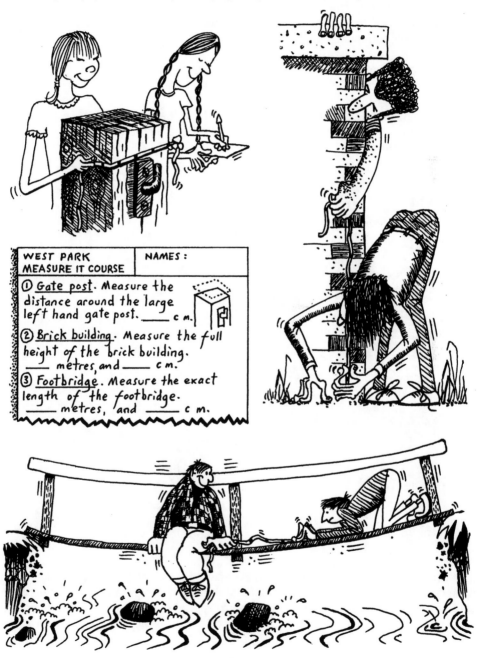

WEST PARK MEASURE IT COURSE	NAMES :

① <u>Gate post</u>. Measure the distance around the large left hand gate post. _____ c m.

② <u>Brick building</u>. Measure the full height of the brick building. _____ metres, and _____ c m.

③ <u>Footbridge</u>. Measure the exact length of the footbridge. _____ metres, and _____ c m.

THE SWEET CHASE

The layout of this event is the same as a normal orienteering 'score' course, but the competitors have an additional bonus at each control site - a sweet!

The red and white control flags or markers are set out around the start/finish area. The controls which are further away from the start are given a higher points value than controls nearer the start. Competitors have complete freedom to work out their own route around the controls. They should visit as many control sites as possible in order to accumulate maximum points in the time allowed.

To make the event even more competitive and exciting, a sweet is hung at each control site. A few larger 'goodies' could be hung at random control sites.

The controls should be set out in such a way that from the mass start there are numerous approaches that can be taken, and the competitors hopefully will split up and aim for different control sites.

Those who reach the control first will find a sweet hanging off the flag or marker, but they will need to show the wrappers as evidence at the finish in order to gain a bonus 50 points. Unlucky competitors who reach a control site after the sweet has been removed will still gain some points by writing down the code letter or punching their control card.

BIKES

Real cycle orienteering presents many organisational problems, e.g. is there a suitable area nearby? Will the landowners give us permission? How do we get the bikes to the event? Do we have enough bikes? How large an area do we need? What sort of map will be needed?

The following exercise attempts to overcome some of the practical problems by scaling down the nature of the event.

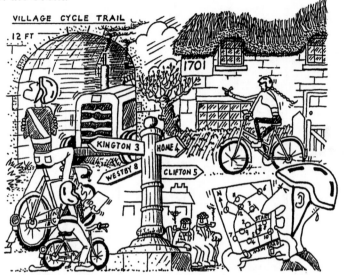

Logistics
1. A local village, with quiet roads and back streets, can make an ideal venue without the need to seek permission from landowners.
2. Simple observation questions could be set at say 10 or 15 points. This method avoids the need to set out control flags.
3. A large scale, clearly drawn street map will be needed, with control points circled and numbered.
4. The cyclists may visit the controls in a given order, or a free choice of route maybe preferred, depending on the particular circumstances.

Safety
1. Most groups will need official approval or authorisation before cycling can proceed.
2. As this exercise is intended to take place on village roads and streets, there will always be unexpected dangers from other vehicles. Rules and safety precautions must be strictly observed.
3. Racing is *not* necessary. Emphasis should be on safe, careful cycling, alone, or in pairs.
4. Groups should be small. There should not be more than seven cyclists to one leader.
5. All cycles should be checked by the leader to see if they are in a roadworthy condition. NOTE: BMX bikes are *not* suitable for this activity.
6. Helmets must be worn.

WINDOW SCORE EXERCISE

This is an interesting way of using a small, well known area for basic orienteering practice. As shown in the example below, only a small part of the map is shown in the 'window' around each control. Sufficient detail is given inside the windows to allow students to navigate between controls. The exercise is mainly intended to practice direct navigation, using compass bearings and pacing, so it would be necessary to check that there are no major obstacles or hazards in between the windows.

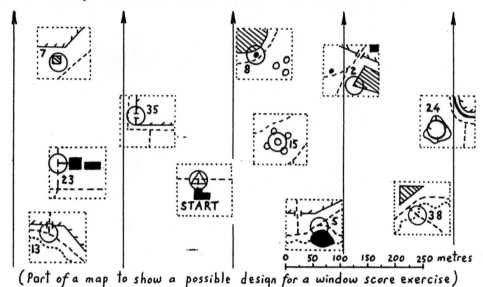

(Part of a map to show a possible design for a window score exercise)

Simple cardboard markers could be made by the group for this training exercise. Their initials could be used as code letters.

This is also designed as a 'score' exercise, which means that competitors should aim to score as may points as possible in a given time limit by visiting the controls in any order.

The controls which are further away from the start should be given a higher points value than the controls nearer the start. There is no set course or order of controls, so competitors are faced with the additional problem of choosing their own route. The whole group may be started at the same time.

NOTE: Competitors will also need a control description list, with points and spaces to write down the code letters. This exercise is based on Tony Thornley's *Window Orienteering* Training Event, as shown in O-Tech Sheet No. 1, published by the British Orienteering Federation.

LOCAL EVENTS

Most of the training events in this chapter are intended to lead up to local events organised by orienteering clubs in your region. Local events normally offer a variety of courses, ranging in difficulty from the easy short courses for beginners to the more demanding longer courses for experienced orienteers. These courses are normally colour coded according to the level of difficulty, with the white and yellow courses being the easiest. People can usually turn up on the day and enter for these events.

Permanent Orienteering Courses

These are rapidly gaining in popularity throughout the regions. They provide a valuable training resource for orienteers of all ages and standards. Further details about permanent orienteering courses can be obtained from *Compass Sport Magazine, Permanent Course Information, 37 Sandycombe Road, Twickenham, Middlesex TW1 2LR.* NOTE: Not all permanent course areas are suitable for beginners. Some areas are extensive, complex and exposed.

To find out more about orienteering and events in your area, send for the general information pack from: British Orienteering Federation, Riversdale, Dale Road North, Darley Dale, Matlock, Derbyshire, DE4 2HX

NIGHT EVENTS

Many orienteering clubs organise night events or training exercises in the winter evenings. This type of orienteering is great fun, and very challenging. It is advisable to check with the organiser, before the event, to see if they can cope with the numbers in your group. It is also advisable to invite only the students who have had some previous orienteering experience, as these night events are normally much more demanding.

NOTE: Leaders must have considerable personal experience of night orienteering. Risk assessments should be carefully considered in some areas where particular hazards and dangers are known.

CAMP ACTIVITIES

In This Chapter

This chapter offers a few ideas which may be fun to do on camp, after the day's activity has been completed. Some pages are intended as preparation exercises for the camp. These include MENU PLANNING, WHAT'S WRONG?, and EXPEDITION CAMP. Some of the activities in this chapter could be included in a camp crafts course, and are therefore suitable for groups working at or near to the base, in the weeks leading up to a planned camp.

Teamwork and co-operation are always important on camp, and so several team problem-solving tasks have been included which are intended to test these qualities. These tasks include TENT PITCHING, FLY SHEET and POCKET JACKET.

Exercises such as MONSTER STORY, CAMP FIRE MUSIC and BIVOUACS are open to the leader's own interpretation, so little or no explanation has been given. Indeed all of the ideas in this book may need to be modified or improved to make them suitable for any particular group or situation.

Planning and Safety

In addition to the general guidelines in Chapter One, the following points are specifically concerned with camping.

- Take great care over all aspects of hygiene, including food preparation, sterile surfaces, sterilised pots and pans, and storage.
- Remind staff and participants that foods need to be thoroughly cooked.
- Check that water supplies are clean.
- Arrange for efficient disposal of waste.
- Encourage good habits of personal cleanliness.
- Inspect tents regularly.
- Brief all participants on out of bounds areas and emergency fire procedures.
- Provide adequate fire extinguishing equipment, especially for large-scale standing camps.
- Note that some disposable gas cylinders may be unsafe for young people to use without close supervision.
- Allow only competent adults to change gas cylinders.
- Check that gas supplies are turned off at the end of each day.
- Ensure that gas cylinders are stored safely and are not exposed to excessive heat.
- Train participants in the safe use of stoves, especially primus and methylated spirit stoves. This training may need to be carried out at the base before the camp begins.
- Be especially careful over the transport of fuels, either in rucksacks for lightweight camping expeditions, or in the minibus/trailer.
- Take special care over interpretation of manufacturer's instructions for multi-fuel/burn-all stoves.
- Space tents to prevent fire from spreading.
- Understand the fire hazards of tent fabrics.
- Be aware of escape routes in the event of fire.
- Have regular roll calls to check that all participants are present.
- For groups undertaking lightweight camping expeditions, be sure to leave details of your route with a responsible adult.

- Especially on camp when groups are living and working together in a rural area for an extended period of time, ensure that the COUNTRY CODE is strictly followed and all participants respect the way of life of local communities.

Recommended Training and Qualifications

Leaders need to be fully aware of the distinctions between various methods of camping and the implications for skills training. For example, a low level camp may be a heavyweight fixed site provision or a lightweight mobile set-up. High level expedition camping obviously requires a much greater level of training. Bivouac or shelter construction may be included in this section and requires totally different skills to those encountered in traditional camping situations. Some adventure centres advertise survival training which includes shelter construction.

Camp leaders and other staff involved should be knowledgeable and experienced so that in the event of problems or emergencies, they are capable of dealing safely with situations. Appropriate training for low-level camping skills can usually be acquired through in-service courses organised by Local Authorities.

The *Summer Mountain Leader Award* provides evidence of competence in high level expedition camping, hillwalking and navigation.

These should be sufficient staff on camp with first aid training.

Publications, Organisations and Addresses

Safety in Outdoor Education, Dept. for Education, HMSO, 1989
This includes a detailed list of publications and addresses.
Camping Guidelines (leaflet), Nottinghamshire County Council - Education, 1993

Outdoor Adventure, exciting open-air activities for youth organisations, David Saint, Printforce Practical Publications, ISBN 0-948834-50-1
Wide Games, Incident Hikes and Indoor Alternatives, David Saint, Printforce Practical Publications, ISBN 0-948834-35-8
More Than Activities, Roger Greenaway, Adventure Education, Penrith, ISBN 1-870322-21-5, 1991

The Cub Scout Handbook, Andrew Pearson, ISBN 0-85165-192-5, 1985, from:
- **The Scout Association**, Baden-Powell house, Queen's Gate, London, SW7 5JS

Duke of Edinburgh's Award Handbook, edited by Nicholas Gair, ISBN 0-905425-02-2
Duke of Edinburgh's Award Expedition Guide, 1988
- both available from **Duke of Edinburgh's Award**, 5 Prince of Wales Terrace, Kensington, London W8 5PG

The SAS Survival Handbook, John Wiseman, Collins Harvill, ISBN 0-00-217185-6, 1986

MENU PLANNING

Plan your menu *for a 3 day camp,*

and estimate the costs.

SHOP AND AUCTION

Both of these exercises are intended to give the group first-hand experience of handling a variety of equipment and clothing usually found in a camping shop.

Camping Shop
Two participants take on the role of shop assistants, and another group member is required to be a customer who will come into the shop and ask for advice on one or two pieces of equipment. The shop assistants must then be as convincing as possible, giving the customer all the usual sales talk. The customer could be the awkward type, who needs to know all about the equipment before he will decide.

Camping Auction
Volunteers take turns at acting as auctioneer. A starting bid is agreed upon and the rest of the group must raise a hand to increase the bid. The auctioneer should aim to point out some of the qualities of the equipment, and try to keep up the fast speaking style.

SPAMBURGERS

The idea for this page came from the practice of giving rewards for good effort or good behaviour when working with small groups of problem youths around an urban base. After several successful sessions with a group, the stove and frying pan would come out of the store room for a well deserved treat, which may be in the form of hot dogs, bacon sandwiches, spamburgers or simply a nice cup of tea! This occasional routine tends to be well appreciated, even if it is sometimes used as a 'carrot'! It also provides a useful focus for communication.

TENT PITCHING

Tent pitching can be made into a group problem solving activity. The exercise can be good fun, and the problem will make people think! NOTE: A more formal approach is recommended for expedition preparation where safety of the group may depend on correct instruction.

Procedure
1. Give each group a tent that is strange to them, and give instructions to pitch the tent correctly, working as a team.
2. State that grades A - E will be given for teamwork, thoroughness in pitching the tent, and effort in packing away.
3. A word about the cost of the tent may be necessary to avoid any damage.
4. When all tents have been pitched, the whole group, with the leader, can inspect each tent in turn, giving criticisms and credit where appropriate.

NOTE: If this exercise is to be successful, it is important that the staff involved have all had personal experience of pitching the same types of tent.

POCKET JACKET

This is an amusing problem solving exercise which will take about one hour. The idea is to design and make a waistcoat with pockets to carry as many items as possible, i.e. tins, potatoes, apples, etc. Teams of 3 or 4 people could work secretly in separate places, and finally 'model' the finished garment in front of the others and the judges.

Equipment needed for each item
Strong polythene sheet
Scissors
Marker pen
Improvised needle
String
Items, e.g. tins, potatoes, apples

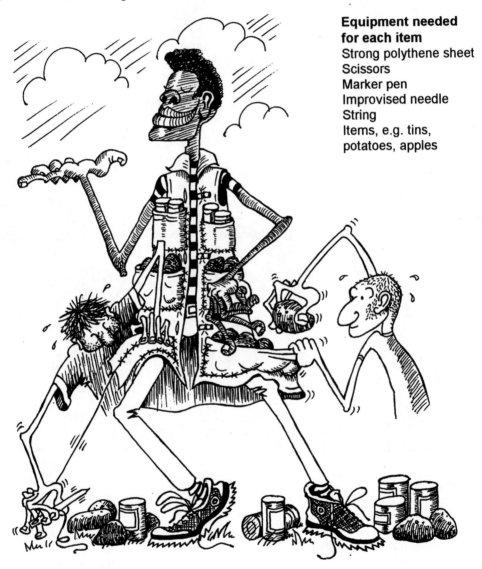

Assessment: Give grades A - E for:

Teamwork
Design
Practical Skills
Holding Capacity of Pockets

WHAT'S WRONG?

(inside the tent)

What should be the correct way?

EXPEDITION CAMP?

This group have just arrived at their expedition camp after a long day on the hill. The site they have chosen is in a remote valley at about 500 metres above sea level. It is late autumn, and weather conditions are becoming worse, with strong winds, and heavy rain clouds approaching.

What are they doing wrong?
What should the correct way be?
What is wrong with their equipment?
What equipment should they use for high level expeditions?
What problems are they likely to face tonight?

PRISONER

The escaped prisoners will need plenty of space to hide within a radius of about 20 metres. Suitable locations could include woodlands, open bracken areas with large boulders, or open common land with many small land forms such as hollows, mounds and small valleys, etc.

Rules of the Game

1. The group is divided into 'prisoners' and 'guards'.
2. Everyone starts at the central point or prison. This could be a definite feature, such as a ruined building, or a circle made from stones.
3. The guards cover their eyes for 30 seconds to allow the prisoners to escape and hide.
4. After 30 seconds, the leader signals for the guards to come out of the prison and search for the escaped prisoners. The guards may search for periods of say 30 seconds. When a prisoner is caught, they should be led back to prison, where they must stay, unless another prisoner reaches in to touch them.
5. The guards will need to decide how many to send out searching.
6. The game continues until all prisoners are caught, then the teams change over.

NOTE: **Beware** of hazards in the area such as sharp branches, hidden rocks and dangerous holes, etc.

THE SENTRY GAME

The sentry game is always a popular evening exercise on camp. There can be many variations to this game, depending on the features available in the area. The basic rules are as follows:

1. Two teams are decided: one team is on sentry duty, and the other team is on a spying mission.
2. The spies are given a white wool arm band at the start of the game.
3. The spy team has to move along a set linear route, i.e. a wall, ditch, hedge, etc. without being caught by the sentry team.
4. The sentry team can only look for the spies at a given interval, i.e. 30 seconds.
5. The sentry team then has another time limit, of say 30 seconds, to locate as many spies as possible, and remove their wool arm bands to prove that they have been caught.

This game can bring out a number of dubious qualities in the youngsters (and the leaders!) but it can mainly be taken as a light-hearted exercise, requiring team co-operation, self-control, concentration and cunning. One of my most successful attempts at this game was on a particularly dark November night in the Derbyshire hills. The linear route chosen was a dry stone wall, and the only way through for the sentry team was via a sheep hole, only one metre high. Our group of rogues became so involved that the game continued well into the night, and the leaders' spy team (who had sportingly agreed to take part) ended up with more than their arm bands removed!

CAMP FIRE MUSIC

SARDINES

This is guaranteed to provide lasting memories. An element of surprise is required for the success of the operation.

When the group are inside their tents, and preparing for a normal night under canvas, the leader announces a change of plan! Everyone should bring their sleeping bags and torches, etc. for a night exercise. The group is then led to an interesting location for a 'sleep out' under the sky. Everyone sleeps side by side, like sardines in a tin. Boys are directed to one site, and girls to a separate site nearby.

Remember to check the weather forecast before the sleep out, and remember to bring a hat - to keep the insects off. Do not sleep inside a plastic survival bag!

FLY SHEET

This is a useful exercise to test group co-operation and communication. The activity is also great fun to watch.

Procedure
1. Each team of four people is given a fly sheet, poles and pegs (or tent, poles and pegs).
2. Instructions are given for two people in the team to be blindfolded, and the other 2 people are to communicate how to erect the fly sheet, without actually helping.
3. The leader awards grades A - E for co-operation, communication and thoroughness.
4. A further grade may be awarded for packing up.

BIVOUACS

Some excellent advice on building various forms of shelter is given in John Wiseman's *SAS Survival Handbook*. Tepees are essentially attractive shelters and of course have strong links with ethnic traditions of many nomadic people, including gypsies and original North Americans. Experiment with your group to produce unusual bivouac designs.

Special care of the environment will be necessary when constructing bivouacs or shelters. No live branches or other vegetation should be cut or uprooted, and the site should be left without any sign of activity or litter after the shelters have been removed.

MONSTER STORY

Book News!!!!!

Peak District Monsters is a fictitious collection of stories, including The Mam Tor Mummy, The Bleaklow Bog-Bouncer and The Dovedale Deadhead, written and illustrated by Alan Smith and published in 1994 by: Trail Crest Publications Ltd, Milne House, Speedwell Mill, Millers Green, Wirksworth, Derbyshire DE4 4BL (ISBN 1-8744754)

DUGLA BALL

This game was invented in the Nepalese village of Dugla by the Australian mountaineer and expedition leader, Terry Ryan. With imagination and a sense of fair play, it can be played:

- with a minimum of equipment
- on almost any (reasonably flat and firm) terrain
- at camp sites anywhere in the world.

Equipment	Value
tennis ball	fun
2 poles about 1 metre high	fair play
(Originally ice axes were used.)	team spirit
rope or string to go between the two poles	'making the most' of limited resources

Procedure: A court is marked out with string, sweaters, scraping your boot along the ground or any other environmentally friendly means. Dimensions vary, but a half a tennis court works well for 4-a-side. A net is erected across the middle with poles and string.

The game is derived from handball and volleyball. Players can stand anywhere on the court. One player serves from the back right corner by knocking the ball with their palm over the net to bounce in the back right corner of the opposing court. The receiving team are allowed three hits, with any part of their body, before the ball must be returned to the serving team. They then have three hits to get it back over the net in turn. Any side failing to do this, or hitting the ball outside the opponent's court, loses the point. No player may hit the ball more than once in succession. The number of bounces allowed between each hit by players on the same side can be one or two, depending on the number of players and the quality of the terrain. The server continues to serve until they lose a point. When the receiving team loses a point they rotate so that a new player receives. If they win a point, one of their team serves. Players take it in turn to serve. *Scoring:* Points are only scored by the serving team. The winners are the first to an agreed number, say nine.

NOTE: a sense of fair play should prevail about the bounce on the serve. Generally, the World Dugla Ball Federation (FIDBA) suggests that the first bounce after the serve must bounce fairly, or the serve is retaken. But other odd bounces are part of the game: hence the slogan of Dugla Ball players everywhere when faced with adversity: "We don't mind."

Challenge: Anyone wishing to stage an Ashes Series against Terry Ryan should contact: FIDBA (UK), 3 Russell House, Lym Close, Lyme Regis, Dorset DT7 3HE. Terry is currently busy trying to establish his other invention, Glacier Cricket, in his boyhood home in the Australian desert! But he wants to hear from new Dugla Ball players, and will respond to all reasonable challenges, which will be forwarded to him promptly.

CREATIVE OUTDOOR WORK

PROBLEM SOLVING

Problem Solving Method

Problem solving as an activity in its own right has taken off remarkably over recent years. Numerous organisations and groups have realised the enormous potential of these activities in various training situations. Schools, outdoor centres and training establishments (including management training) have taken on board problem solving tasks with their groups. Through carefully planned exercises, appropriate to the participants, young people can work together in a positive manner with realistic targets to meet.

Problem solving provides opportunities for participants to cope with unusual situations. To be successful problem solvers they must show some initiative, and be resourceful. The exercises in this chapter have been selected because of their appeal to young people.

A method of approaching problem solving is shown on the opposite page. I have found the two most important aspects to be 'working as a team' and 'persevering'. Ability for 'lateral thinking' is also a useful asset.

Problem solving may be done in many situations. It may be planned as an activity in a residential centre or camp. It may be used on a training course at the base, or as an evening fun session when the day's activities have been completed.

Each individual leader will have his or her particular way of introducing an exercise to the group. A suggested way is to give the group a brief look at the sketch to help motivate the participants. The leader would then need to describe the problem, and hand out the equipment. The teams may then continue without further reference to the sketch, although the leader will need to be at hand to give encouragement. The easiest option in problem solving situations is to give up! For more experienced groups, it may be sufficient to describe the problem briefly, without reference to the sketch. Participants should always aim to experiment and try alternative solutions.

Assessment: Some of the stages used with problem solving, as shown on the next page, may be used as a basis for assessing the students. A grade A, B, C, D or E could be given for each stage to be assessed.

The Stages of Problem Solving

Here are some stages which are intended to be used with each of the problem solving exercises in this chapter.

PLANNING AND DESIGNING

CONSIDERING ALTERNATIVES

WORKING AS A TEAM

USING SKILLS AND KNOWLEDGE

PERSEVERING

TESTING

MODIFYING

TIDYING

REFLECTING

Assessment

Some of these stages may be used as a basis for asessing the students.
A grade A, B, C, D or E could be given for each stage to be assessed.

Levels of Difficulty

The activities outlined here are not intended to show the only way of solving problems. Leaders and participants are encouraged to adapt and improve on these basic ideas.

Bearing in mind the limited range of work outlined in this book, it may be helpful to identify three levels of difficulty for these problem solving exercises.

Level One: Straightforward, basic tasks requiring few essential skills, but involving teamwork and perseverance for successful results. Examples include:

OBSTACLE RELAY
MINI ASSAULT COURSE
CANDLE LANTERNS
POTATO CONVEYOR
MODEL CARGO BOATS
SHADUF
BRICKHENGE

Level Two: More technical tasks, requiring skills preparation, i.e. tying knots, using a map scale, taking compass bearings, etc. Safety considerations and levels of responsibility or maturity are involved. Examples include:

FLYING MESSAGE
STILES
QUICK-HAMMOCKS
WATER TRANSPORTER
CARRY SEATS
SIGN POSTS

Level Three: Demanding multi-problem tasks, possibly requiring several days or weeks of planning, training and organisation. Safety considerations are essential and all the stages suggested earlier in this chapter are involved. These tasks are likely to be undertaken off-site in unusual surroundings. Examples include:

> ALL NIGHT PROBLEMS
> STRETCHERS (See Chapter 3)
> NIGHT NAVIGATION (See Chapter 3)

Some leaders may prefer to assess their students on their problem solving skills, and others may do it just for fun. There is room for both approaches. Some of the stages illustrated earlier in this chapter could be drawn up into a grid, and used as an assessment record sheet, so that leaders and participants may follow their progress over a period of time.

Finally, don't forget the camera or video recorder! Participants will enjoy looking at their problem solving capers captured on film.

Equipment

Most of the basic equipment required for these exercises is easily obtainable from hardware or DIY stores. The **wooden poles** could be purchased through your Area Forestry Commission office, or from a garden centre. The poles do not need to be too thick and heavy for the exercises in this chapter; a maximum diameter of 7cm should be sufficient. Hard woods will obviously last longer than soft woods. the poles will also be useful for other exercises in this book, e.g. BIVOUACS and STRETCHERS.

None of the exercises here will require any great strain on the **ropes** or lines. A recommended thin strong rope for lashing light poles together, and for other purposes, including the overhead rope in the WATER TRANSPORTER exercise and the main support ropes in QUICK HAMMOCKS, is an 8mm diameter, 3-strand hawser laid terylene rope. Lashing ropes for use with the light poles may be cut up into lengths of 5 or 6 metres with their ends sealed to prevent fraying.

The exercises are likely to be more successful if some time is spent practising **knots**. Useful knots to learn include:

> square lashing
> diagonal lashing
> reef knot
> bowline
> overhand loop
> figure of eight loop
> round turn and two half hitches.

The Scouts have been problem solving (or 'pioneering') or many years. John Sweet's *Scout Pioneering* book, obtainable from camping and outdoor shops, contains a wealth of useful information on knots, equipment and exercises and is fully illustrated. This book is highly recommended for leaders who intend to develop their problem solving or pioneering.

Planning and Safety

Much of the general advice given in Chapter One will apply to Problem Solving work. From experience with various groups attempting these tasks, the following points are also worth considering:

- Be vigilant over correct use of equipment.
- Be aware of individuals going too far out of the brief.
- Be prepared, if necessary, to step in if conflicts arise.
- Stress safety points which apply to each task.
- Assess hazards in surrounding area.
- Give advice on correct methods of lifting and carrying heavy items.
- Plan problems within limitations of all participants.
- Fully brief all staff or helpers.
- Ensure adequate supervision is present
- Agree on a communication system between staff, and decide appropriate time limits, especially if several groups are involved.

Training and Qualifications

As far as I am aware, there is no specific training or qualification for problem solving as yet. This is understandable due to the diversity of possibilities. Leaders who are responsible for creating problem solving tasks may find the three levels of difficulty in this introduction of some guidance as they consider appropriate ideas.

Many of the basic skills required by staff could well be acquired by working with other leaders or through in-service training. For the more demanding problem solving tasks outlined in Level Three, the *Summer Mountain Leader Award* or the British Orienteering Federation *Orienteering Instructor Award* can be recommended, especially when difficult navigation decisions are to be encountered in hilly areas or at night.

Publications

The New Youth Games Book, Alan Dearling and Howie Armstrong with illustrations by Jerry Neville, Russell House Publishing Ltd, 38 Silver Street, Lyme Regis, Dorset, DT7 3HS, ISBN 1-898924-00-7, 1994
Adventure Education - Bookshop and Training Resource Catalogue, available from Adventure Education, 39 Brunswick Square, Penrith, Cumbria CA11 7LS
City Adventure, David Rose, Paul Chapman Publishing Ltd, ISBN 1-85396-048-9, 1989
Silver Bullets: A Guide to Initiative Problems, Adventure Games and Trust Activities, Karle Rohnke, Kendall/Hunt Publishing Co., Iowa, ISBN 08403-5682-X, 1984
Scout Pioneering, John Sweet, The Scouts Association, 1986

OBSTACLE RELAY

The Problem: To design and construct an obstacle course.

Each team should include 15 problems in their obstacle course. All courses should be about the same length. Each problem should be designed so that a blinfolded competitor can successfully move along the course with a member of his or her team giving instructions from behind a line. Possible problems could include:

stepping over	squeezing through
crawling under	changing direction
stepping between	picking up items
carrying items, etc.	

When the obstacle courses have been constructed and tested, teams change over courses, and all members attempt to complete the course in turn. One person from each team will be needed to judge and mark down penalty points for each fault. The game may be organised as a relay, with times recorded for all competitors, and seconds added on for the number of faults.

Equipment needed for each team

pencil and paper	bamboo canes
string	scissors
large polythene sheet	wooden tent pegs
mallet	clip board
watch	blindfold

MINI ASSAULT COURSE

The Problem: To design, and attempt to complete, a miniature assault course, using only the natural features which are already present.

The area should ideally contain a grassy slope (not too steep!), a few large fallen trees, some trees with strong lower branches for climbing (not higher than say 8 feet) and a few hollows or earth mounds. A typical course could include some of the following features:

> balance along a fallen tree,
> jump over a hollow,
> run up a grassy slope,
> crawl through a hollow tree trunk,
> hop over some low earth mounds,
> snake under some low branches,
> climb up a tree to about 8ft, then move along a strong branch and drop down,
> and zigzag through some trees to finish.

Safety

This exercise is meant to be an *easy* version of an army assault course. The leader will need to lay down strict rules, to make clear the exact area to be used, the maximum height to be climbed, the maximum distance to jump, and any other specific safety points. All students should wear training shoes and old clothes. At least two adults are recommended for a maximum group size of ten. Be sure to choose a suitable area with public access.

FLYING MESSAGE

The Problem: To send a flying message (without throwing!) over a line which has been raised 12 feet above the ground.

A suggested method is illustrated below, but note that this task can be more fun if each team devises a different solution to the problem, e.g. catapult, glider, launcher, etc.

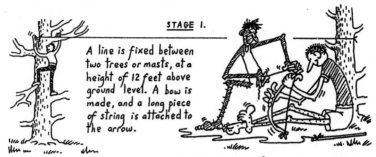

STAGE I.

A line is fixed between two trees or masts, at a height of 12 feet above ground level. A bow is made, and a long piece of string is attached to the arrow.

STAGE 2.
Following the leader's strict safety rules, the archer should aim to fire the arrow and string over the high line, and into a 6 foot diameter circle – which has been marked out on the grass. Part of the problem is to work out a method of keeping the string free from tangles as it runs out. A quick and easy method of retrieving the arrow and string (without using the bow), will also need to be considered.

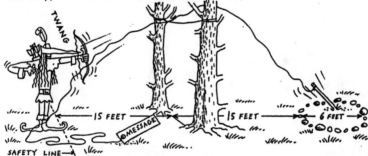

TWANG

IS FEET — IS FEET — 6 FEET

MESSAGE

SAFETY LINE

STAGE 3. Only when the arrow lands inside the circle, can another member of the team move to the circle, and pull the string (with a message attached) over the high line and into the circle.

Equipment needed for each team

overhead line
smooth straight stick for arrow
pen knife
message

bendy stick for bow
long length of thin string (at least 50ft)
small hacksaw

Safety

All members of the team (and spectators) should remain behind the safety line when the arrow is fired. If more than one team is engaged in the same exercise, then a safe distance between the teams should be decided. One adult per team is recommended. Avoid areas with overhead power lines!

CANDLE LANTERNS

The problem: To design and construct a lantern, containing a candle, using only the equipment listed below. The lantern should be designed so that the lighted candle would not blow out in breezy conditions, and the shield would not catch fire. The final problem is to see which team can carry the lighted lantern, attached to the top of a long cane, for a distance of 50 metres out of doors.

Equipment needed for each team

pencil and paper
polythene sheet
string
bendy wire
hacksaw
candle

several short bamboo or garden canes
scissors
tape
wire cutters
matches
long bamboo cane

STILES

The problem: To design and construct a temporary stile over a fence or wall. This exercise provides opportunity for design, knot tying skills and teamwork. Permission from the landowner may be required. Care should be taken to avoid any damage to the fence or wall.

Equipment needed for each team

strong wooden poles of various lengths
strong lashing ropes
pencil and paper

QUICK HAMMOCKS

The Problem:
Session 1: practise your knots on these quick hammocks.
Session 2: design and construct your own hammock or swing chair.

Safety Points
- No pushing!
- Leader to check all knots and supports.
- Height - not more than 5 feet above the ground.

Assessment
Give grades A - E for: teamwork
                          knot tying skills
                          tidying

Quick Hammock A
Make fast to support posts with bowlines or round turn and two half hitches.

Equipment needed   main support ropes
                        strong polythene sheet or canvas
                        4 support posts or trees

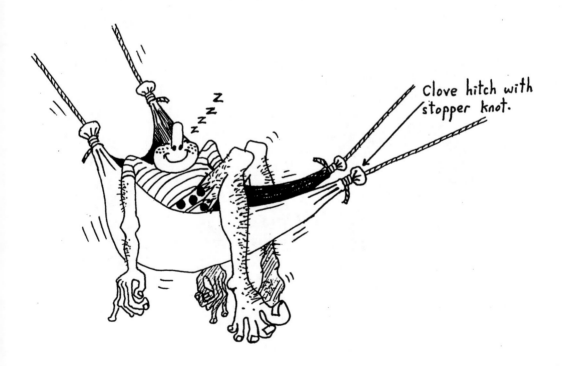

Clove hitch with stopper knot.

Quick Hammock B

Equipment needed   main support ropes
strong polythene sheet or canvas
2 support posts or trees

Quick Hammock C

This method will probably take two students between one and two hours to construct.

Equipment needed   main support ropes
strong lashing ropes for making net
2 wooden poles

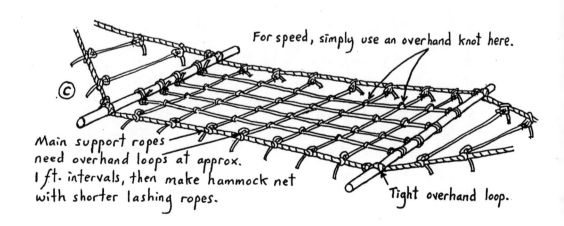

For speed, simply use an overhand knot here.

Main support ropes need overhand loops at approx. 1 ft. intervals, then make hammock net with shorter lashing ropes.

Tight overhand loop.

POTATO CONVEYOR

The problem: To design and construct a structure for a potato (or tennis ball) to roll down by gravity.

The journey taken by the potato should be as interesting as possible. There should be at least two main bends and a drop along the route. Points may be awarded for design, teamwork, practical skills, length of journey, and time in seconds for the journey. The longest time gains the most points!

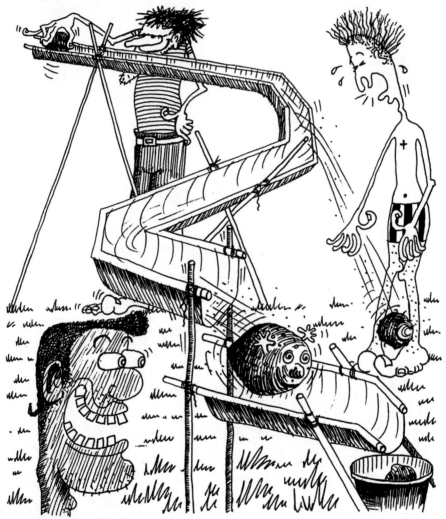

Equipment needed for each team

pencil and paper
hacksaw
string
short length of tape

bamboo canes
strips of polythene
scissors
one round potato or tennis ball

MODEL CARGO BOATS

The Problem: To design and construct a model boat, which should be stable enough to carry a given cargo. Each pair may choose one of the following types of boat to construct:

catamaran	trimaran
canoe with outrigger	raft
coracle	cargo boat
punt	

The maximum length of the model boat should be no more than one metre.
Sails are optional.

A section of stream, preferably with a small rapid and a bend, should be chosen to test the finished models. Small plastic bags filled with sand or pebbles may be used for the cargo. The winning boat will be the one to carry the cargo bags over the set distance without capsizing.

Equipment needed

pencil and paper	bamboo canes
bendy sticks	hacksaw
string	scissors
polythene sheet	tape
glue	various scraps of wood
long canes for rescuing drifting boats	cargo bags
small plastic containers (e.g. washing-up liquid type)	

WATER TRANSPORTER

The Problem: To transport a bucket of water across a stream at a height of 8 feet above the ground, using an overhead rope system. Each team must transport the suspended bucket of water along the overhead rope system to the other side of the stream, without actually touching the bucket.

The winning team will present the bucket which contains the most water. NOTE: protective wrapping should be used around trees on both sides of the stream.

Equipment needs or each team

overhead rope
sisal twine
large bucket

protective wrapping for trees
scissors
small container (for filling the bucket)

karabiner for suspending the bucket (available from most camping shops)

Safety

This exercise is only intended for shallow streams, using only a bucket of water on an overhead rope system. The leader should check the security of the rope system before the bucket is transported. Recommended knots for securing the overhead rope are: bowlines, or round turn and two half hitches.

SHADUF

A shaduf is a primitive method of raising water from a river to irrigation ditches. The structure, using poles and bucket, has been used for centuries in Egypt along the banks of the Nile.

The Problem: To design and construct a shaduf. The structure will be free-standing, using a tripod or similar method, and the bucket will be attached to a long pole which pivots at the apex of the tripod. By applying weight to the long pole, the bucket (or container) may be raised, lowered, or moved from side to side.

The final problem, which is best done as a team race, is to see how much water can be raised from a stream or river, and tipped into another bucket on the bank side, in a time of say 3 minutes.

Equipment needed for each team

6 x 7ft poles	lengths of lashing rope
ball of string	scissors
large bucket	small bucket or container

CARRY SEATS

The Problem: To design and construct a contraption with a seat for carrying a person. The finished product should be safe for the passenger, even when transported in a carry seat race! This exercise is intended for teams of 5 people.

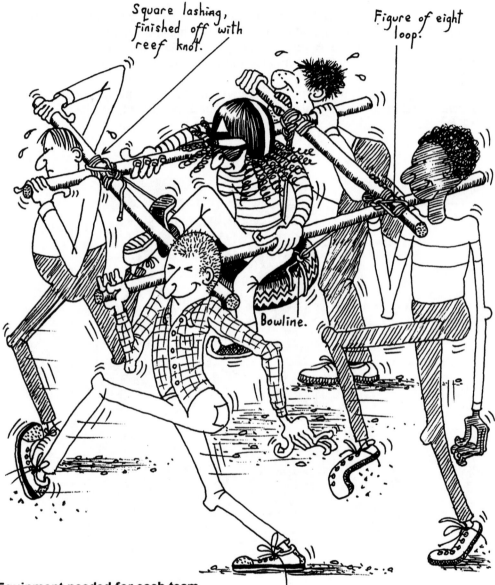

Square lashing, finished off with reef knot.

Figure of eight loop.

Bowline.

Equipment needed for each team
    4 strong wooden poles for the frame
    strong lashing ropes
    old car tyre
    crash helmet (optional)

SIGNPOST

The problem: To design and construct a signpost, which should point to a number of places marked on the map.

This may be done at a suitable point during a walk, or in the grounds at the base. The leader may divide the group into teams and give instructions to build a signpost, using dead sticks from the surrounding area. The completed signpost should point accurately to at least ten villages, or places of interest, and give clear indication of place names, compass directions (e.g. NE) and direct distance in kilometres.

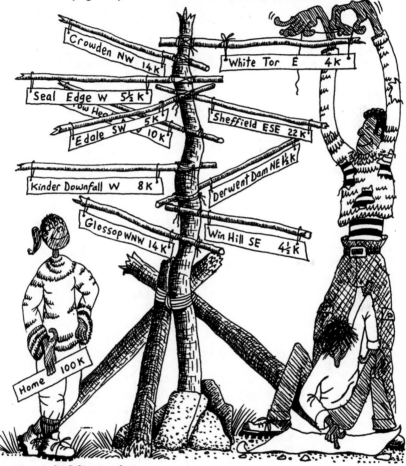

Equipment needed for each team

dead sticks
cardboard strips
marker pens
compass

string or sisal twine
scissors
Ordnance Survey map

This exercise photographs well, both the finished signpost and while it is being made. So a camera is also a good thing to bring along, if possible.

BRICKHENGE

The Problem:

To apply fundamental moving and lifting principles, to construct a miniature Stonehenge, using bricks. The idea is to build the model, using labour saving devices, as shown in the sketches below. The bricks should not be touched by hand at any stage of the exercise.

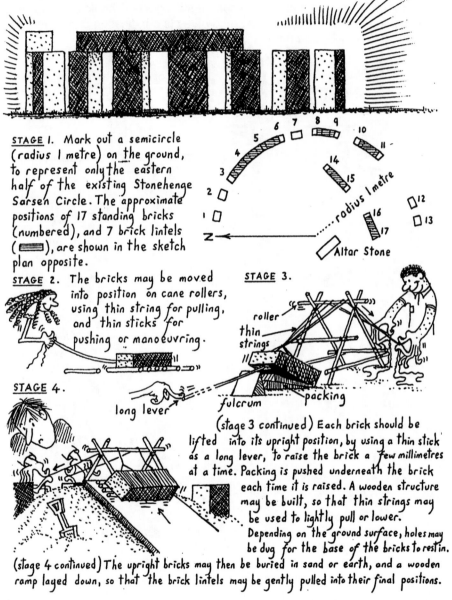

STAGE 1. Mark out a semicircle (radius 1 metre) on the ground, to represent only the eastern half of the existing Stonehenge Sarsen Circle. The approximate positions of 17 standing bricks (numbered), and 7 brick lintels (▭), are shown in the sketch plan opposite.

STAGE 2. The bricks may be moved into position on cane rollers, using thin string for pulling, and thin sticks for pushing or manoeuvring.

STAGE 3.

(stage 3 continued) Each brick should be lifted into its upright position, by using a thin stick as a long lever, to raise the brick a few millimetres at a time. Packing is pushed underneath the brick each time it is raised. A wooden structure may be built, so that thin strings may be used to lightly pull or lower. Depending on the ground surface, holes may be dug for the base of the bricks to rest in.

STAGE 4.

(stage 4 continued) The upright bricks may then be buried in sand or earth, and a wooden ramp layed down, so that the brick lintels may be gently pulled into their final positions.

NOTE: the methods used in this exercise are not necessarily the same methods used in the actual construction of Stonehenge.

ALL NIGHT PROBLEMS

This demanding exercise is intended for participants who have had some experience of orienteering, map and compass training, and camp crafts. Even with an experienced group it would be necessary to hold a number of planning and training meetings with all of the students.

The idea of this exercise is for teams of 2 or 3 participants to navigate through the night in fairly mild countryside, on public paths, bridleways and minor roads. A number of problems are set out at various points throughout the route. The teams attempt to solve each problem and finally navigate to a finish point, where an improvised shelter is to be set up to sleep in.

The NIGHT NAVIGATION exercise in Chapter 3 gives a suggested outline, which may be amended to fit your particular objectives.

A piece of advice for leaders thinking of tackling this exercise is to make sure you have plenty of willing helpers who are prepared to put up with a full night without sleep!

PROCEDURE: ① The teams are timed out at intervals of about 5 minutes, (after an equipment check). ② The teams navigate to a number of orienteering markers which are set out along the route.

③ The teams check in at a few manned controls, and show their control cards.

④ The teams must solve a few problems, at set points along the route; e.g. using a given code system, found in an envelope at a check point, use a torch to flash a coded message (to identify the name of your group?), and receive a coded message, which will be flashed back.

⑤ At the finish point, the teams must construct a shelter to sleep in, using the materials provided. Boys sleep in separate shelters to the girls. A meal is to be cooked, on a stove, or open fire, depending on the location, and experience of the group.

STUDYING THE ENVIRONMENT

In This Chapter

A keen awareness of our environment is fundamental to all aspects of outdoor work, and staff share a considerable responsibility for educating young people so that environmental concerns are foremost in their minds. By studying the environment through a variety of surveys and exercises in the field, an appreciation of our rural and urban landscapes can be developed. In the process a wide range of social and interpersonal skills can also be developed, as is pointed out where appropriate in each of the exercises.

The pages here attempt to show a range of possibilities for looking at the environment with small groups of young people. The cartoons illustrate various methods of recording observations, measuring and estimating distance, and using basic communication skills. Hopefully these exercises are designed so that the work will be interesting and enjoyable. Maximum individual involvement is essential. To encourage this the group may be divided into pairs, each pair having responsibility for completing a number of tasks. The leader or teacher should always be fairly close at hand to give help and encouragement, and to offer guidance.

All participants involved in environmental studies should be fully aware of The Country Code. The CONFLICT exercise in this chapter will help young people to understand some of The Code's implications.

A selection of follow-up exercises has been included at the bottom of most pages in this chapter. They may offer some ideas for developing the work done in the field.

Planning and Safety

Much of the general advice given in Chapter One will apply to environmental studies. The following additional points relate to specific environments often visited for field studies.

- Organise participants to work in small groups or pairs for security and safety reasons.
- Give a clear brief - including where and when to meet, and what to do in an emergency, or if they are late.
- Warn young people about how they approach strangers.
- Visit urban areas in advance to check for hazards.
- Avoid urban areas where conflicts are likely to arise with residents.
- Stress the dangers of road junctions and of crossing roads.
- Keep to public rights of way.
- Be aware of protected plants and animals.
- Keep away from dangerous slopes and cliffs where falling stones could be a hazard.
- Keep off frozen lakes and rivers during winter field studies.
- Carefully choose stream or pond survey sites for safe groupwork.
- Always check high tide times when working in coastal areas.

Training and Qualifications

Teachers will of course have completed Higher Education training in Environmental Studies, Geography, Geology, Biology or other related subjects. But background knowledge, experience and a strong interest in field studies can enable those without such training to become successfully involved in environmental work at a basic level.

In-service training may be necessary for acquiring additional fieldwork skills in specific environments, and the *Summer Mountain Leader Award* would be strongly recommended for field studies in moorland, hills and mountains.

Publications

Safety in Outdoor Education, Dept. for Education, HMSO, 1989
Sharing the Joy of Nature, Joseph Cornell, Dawn Publications,
ISBN 0-9l6124-52-5, 1989
Sharing Nature With Children, Joseph Cornell, Exley Publications,
ISBN 1-85015-137-7, 1989
Get to Know Nature: Project and Activity Ideas for Children, Jean Barrow, Printforce Practical publication, ISBN 0-948834-60-9
Invertebrates: identification in the School Grounds, Lynnette Merrick, Learning Through Landscapes Trust, Southgate Publishers Ltd, ISBN 1-85741-086-6, 1993
Let's Go Green: Environmental Ideas, Activities and Information for Young People, Lora A. Lisbon, Printforce Ltd, ISBN 0-948834-36-6

Organisations

World Wide Fund For Nature
Their Education Catalogue is available from: World Wide Fund For Nature, Publishing Unit, Panda House, Weyside Park, Godalming, Surrey GU7 1XR
Friends of the Earth
26-28 Underwood Street, London N1 7JQ
Greenpeace
Canonbury Villas, London N1 2PN
The Watch Trust for Environmental Education
22 The Green, Nettleham, Lincoln LN2 2NR
Royal Society for the Protection of Birds
The Lodge, Sandy, Bedfordshire
Council for Environmental Education
School of Education, University of Reading, London Road, Reading RG1 5AQ
Field Studies Council
Information Office, Preston Montford, Montford Bridge, Shrewsbury SY4 1HW
Nature Conservancy Council
Northminster House, Peterborough PE1 1VA

Acknowledgement

The idea for LAND FOR DEVELOPMENT is based on a set of Geography teaching materials produced by the Schools Council Development Project Team.

VILLAGE SURVEY

The aim of this survey is to make simple labelled sketches to show the shape, character and use of buildings along a given frontage. The group may be split up into pairs so that sketches may be made of all the interesting parts of the village.

Back at the base, a cardboard stand-up model could be made by cutting out the skyline shapes of the buildings and adding as much colour and detail as possible to capture the real character of the village. The finished model may then form the basis for further investigations, e.g. land use patterns, conservation areas, traffic problems, building structures, etc.

(stand up model)

Value
environmental awareness
aesthetic appreciation
concentration
self discipline
field sketching skills
annotating skills

PUZZLE TRAILS

Puzzle trails are especially suitable for village and town studies. They may be organised in 'street orienteering' style as outlined in Chapter 2. The students will need a map and a list of puzzles to solve. A selection of possible puzzle questions is given below.

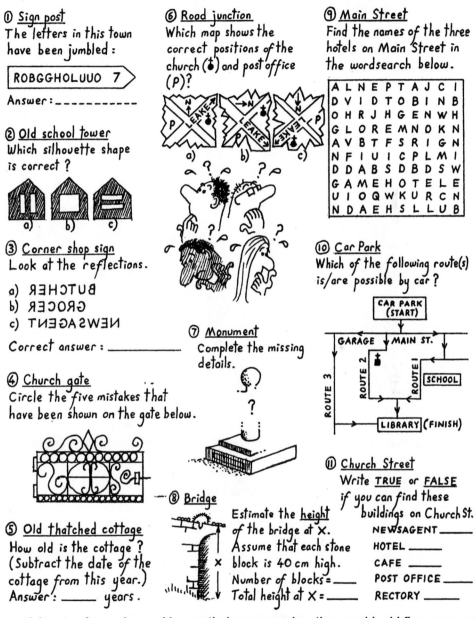

① Sign post
The letters in this town have been jumbled:

ROBGGHOLUUO 7

Answer: _ _ _ _ _ _ _ _ _

② Old school tower
Which silhouette shape is correct?

a)   b)   c)

③ Corner shop sign
Look at the reflections.

a) ЯƎHϽTUꓭ
b) ЯƎϽOЯꓨ
c) TИƎꓨAꙄWƎИ

Correct answer: _ _ _ _ _ _ _

④ Church gate
Circle the five mistakes that have been shown on the gate below.

⑤ Old thatched cottage
How old is the cottage? (Subtract the date of the cottage from this year.)
Answer: _ _ _ _ years.

⑥ Road junction
Which map shows the correct positions of the church (✝) and post office (P)?

a)   b)   c)

⑦ Monument
Complete the missing details.

⑧ Bridge
Estimate the height of the bridge at X. Assume that each stone block is 40 cm high.
Number of blocks = _ _ _
Total height at X = _ _ _

⑨ Main Street
Find the names of the three hotels on Main Street in the wordsearch below.

A	L	N	E	P	T	A	J	C	I
D	V	I	D	T	O	B	I	N	B
O	H	R	J	H	G	E	N	W	H
G	L	O	R	E	M	N	O	K	N
A	V	B	T	F	S	R	I	G	N
N	F	I	U	I	C	P	L	M	I
D	D	A	B	S	D	B	D	S	W
G	A	M	E	H	O	T	E	L	E
U	I	O	Q	W	K	U	R	C	N
N	D	A	E	H	S	L	L	U	B

⑩ Car Park
Which of the following route(s) is/are possible by car?

CAR PARK (START)
GARAGE MAIN ST.
ROUTE 3
ROUTE 2
ROUTE 1
SCHOOL
LIBRARY (FINISH)

⑪ Church Street
Write **TRUE** or **FALSE** if you can find these buildings on Church St.
NEWSAGENT _ _ _ _
HOTEL _ _ _ _
CAFE _ _ _ _
POST OFFICE _ _ _ _
RECTORY _ _ _ _

As participants often enjoy making up their own puzzles, they could add five more puzzle questions to the list as they walk around the trail, and number them on their street map. NOTE: photographs of places or features can also be used in puzzle trails.

STREET INTERVIEWS

An interesting way of collecting information for a local study is to go out into the community with a set of questions that have been worked out in advance. The method of interviewing people in the street provides an unusual and exciting approach for the students who will probably gain much from the experience, if it is done correctly.

The questions could be set to find out about people's shopping habits; about local problems such as traffic or pollution; or about local attitudes to new developments such as a new superstore or factory.

Value
communication with adults
self awareness
self confidence
responsibilities
personal conduct
situation experience
environmental awareness

Some suggestions
- Participants should always be polite, even when people do not want to be interviewed.
- The questionnaire should be easy to use outside. This could mean having questions with short alternative answers to tick.
- Participants may be involved in designing the questionnaire.
- Participants should be given a definite area to work in.
- This exercise is best done in pairs.
- A tape recorder may be used, especially if longer answers or opinions are required.
- Be careful not to overuse this exercise in the same area.
- Alternative surveys should be ready for students who show signs that they cannot cope with the situation.

Follow-up Work
1. Compare results with other participants doing the same survey.
2. Draw up the results of the surveys in the form of maps, graphs or diagrams, and make some conclusions.

ENVIRONMENTAL QUALITY SURVEY

The aim of this survey is to compare the environmental quality in three different areas.

Name of Street: North End Flats						Names: Jill and Wayne					
Show your opinion of the environmental quality of this street by shading the boxes below											
Factors	HIGH QUALITY	←	→	LOW		Factors	HIGH QUALITY	←	→	LOW	
State of repair					▓	Greenery (e.g. trees)					▓
Character of buildings					▓	Surrounding land use				▓	
View from windows	▓					Traffic (safe ← → dangerous)					▓
Daylight through windows		▓				Street lighting	▓				
House entrance designs					▓	Outside noise level					▓
Car space				▓		Air, cleanliness				▓	
Vandalism (lack of ← → much)					▓	Shop access					▓
Privacy					▓	Public transport (eg. bus stops)	▓				
Garden size					▓	Pavements				▓	
Neighbourhood play areas		▓				Other (specify): Entertainment					

Follow-up Work:
1. Rewrite the list of 20 factors in **your** order of importance.
2. Draw suitable graphs or diagrams to show the results of your survey.
3. Write a letter to your local council suggesting realistic ways of improving the environment in your survey area.

NOTE: Be careful not to overuse this survey in the same streets.

OUR NEIGHBOURHOOD PLAN

The aim of this exercise is to design a new neighbourhood centre for one hundred years ahead. The new centre would be based on the site of the existing centre, and may retain some of the chosen existing features. The students should already be familiar with the functions of a neighbourhood centre, with its transport systems and services.

Stage One
A visit to the site will need to be arranged for the group to make a plan showing existing layout and use of buildings, roads and other special features. Each pair of students will need a large scale base map of the road system on to which notes and symbols are to be added.

Stage Two: Designing and Making the Neighbourhood Plan
Different coloured pieces of card may be cut to shape, labelled and positioned on the base map (See below.) to show the new neighbourhood centre design. Card may be used to give a 3-D effect for some features, e.g. flyovers, high level transport systems, and particular buildings.

TEAM ASSESSMENT	
FIELDWORK ROUGH PLANS	20
FIELDWORK EFFORT	20
DESIGN AND ORIGINALITY	20
FINISHED PRODUCT	20
ORAL PRESENTATION	20
TOTAL POINTS	100

Stage Three
Each team should be prepared to talk about their plan to the whole group. This would involve pointing out the main features, giving reasons for aspects of the design, and defending their plans against opposition from critics.

CONFLICT

Simulate a situation where a small group of hikers meet up with a landowner. This may be done in several ways:

1. The bad mannered hikers have gone the wrong way across the landowner's field, and both sides exchange their strong opinions, with the hikers eventually continuing undeterred along their illegal route.
2. The polite group of hikers has gone the correct way across the landowner's field, but the angry landowner turns them back.
3. The polite group of hikers has gone the correct way across the landowner's field. they meet up with the landowner, and both sides sensibly and calmly exchange their views.

NOTE: Participants involved in acting out this situation should show *self control* and *restraint*.

Conclusions

What should be the best way to behave in these situations?
What reasons may the landowner give for turning you off his land?
What polite answers may the hikers give to the landowner?
What would happen if all hikers took no notice of fences, paths and signs?
NOTE: A useful section on access is included in Eric Langmuir's *Mountaincraft and Leadership*.

ENVIRONMENT TRAILS

Environment trails can be worked out on questionnaire style sheets. A set route marked on a sketch map will be required for the students to follow.

Various questions are completed and observations made en route. These could be related to a variety of environmental features, e.g. land use, building styles, map features, plants, land shape, geological features, special features e.g. bridge, dam, wall, lock gate, waterfall. Choose a variety of things to do, to prevent the questions from becoming repetitive.

POINT ① (first field)
What does the farmer use this field for ? (5 points)

POINT ② (old stone barn)
Estimate the area of the barn.
length ___ metres X width___m
= _____ square metres. (15 points)

POINT ③ (path junction)
Use your Ordnance Survey map to find out where the 4 paths lead to. (20 points)

POINT ④ (plantation corner)
Sketch the leaves of 2 different conifer trees, and collect a cone from the ground for your display.

POINT ⑤ (ancient burial mounds)
Make a simple sketch map of the burial mounds, using the symbols provided. (50 points)

RATTLE!

TOTAL POINTS

OUT OF 200

The style of questions or tasks in the field should be designed to allow maximum individual involvement. Small groups, or pairs working on their own, should be encouraged when possible. The role of the leader here should be as a guide who gives suggestions and encouragement, but at the same time allows the participants to think and work out things for themselves.

CREATIVE OUTDOOR WORK

FARMLAND SURVEY

As participants walk along a country lane or track, they may observe the land use on either side of them, and record symbols to make up a simple map. Symbols may also be added to show estimated quality of farmland and type of livestock. A pocket reference book would be useful for students to identify the different types of crops and animals.

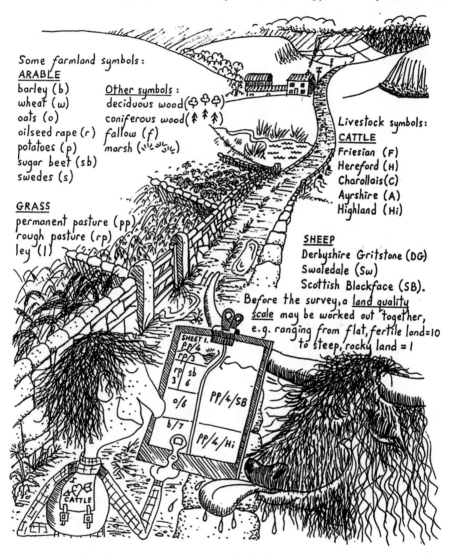

Some farmland symbols:
ARABLE
barley (b)
wheat (w)
oats (o)
oilseed rape (r)
potatoes (p)
sugar beet (sb)
swedes (s)

Other symbols:
deciduous wood
coniferous wood
fallow (f)
marsh

GRASS
permanent pasture (pp)
rough pasture (rp)
ley (l)

Livestock symbols:
CATTLE
Friesian (F)
Hereford (H)
Charollais (C)
Ayrshire (A)
Highland (Hi)

SHEEP
Derbyshire Gritstone (DG)
Swaledale (Sw)
Scottish Blackface (SB).

Before the survey, a land quality scale may be worked out together, e.g. ranging from flat, fertile land=10 to steep, rocky land = 1

SHEET I.
PP/4
rp/3
rp/sb 3/6
o/6
b/7
PP/4/SB
PP/4/Hi

CATTLE

The farmer's permission may be needed for this survey.

Follow-up Work
1. Draw up your land use map using colour and symbols.
2. Try to explain why the farmer has used their fields in this way.
3. Comment on the problems for farming in your survey area.

OBSERVATION GAME

"Okay, Mary and Stan, you are on a spying mission in enemy territory, and you have sixty seconds to use your photographic memories."

The participants are expected to remember as much detail as possible about the view, which may be a panoramic landscape, a village, a farm, or an interesting building. If possible the chosen points for the observation game should be pre-planned, so that the view is hidden as the students approach.

There are several different ways of doing this exercise, depending on the level of difficulty required:
Easiest method: Participants observe and then answer questions orally.
Medium method: Participants observe and then tick off a simple check list.
Hard method: Participants observe and then make a fully labelled sketch from memory.

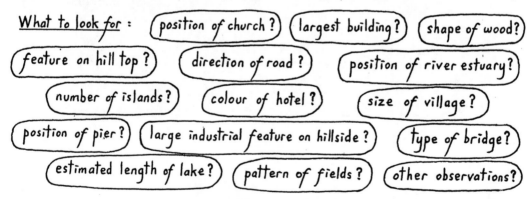

What to look for : position of church? largest building? shape of wood? feature on hill top? direction of road? position of river estuary? number of islands? colour of hotel? size of village? position of pier? large industrial feature on hillside? type of bridge? estimated length of lake? pattern of fields? other observations?

NOTE: Participants would not be expected to do this observation game without some preliminary guidelines, clues and examples.

WINTER BIRD SURVEY

A frozen park lake presents an ideal opportunity for close range bird watching. A bag full of crumbs will make the outing even more rewarding as many wild ducks, geese and swans will readily accept food at very close range when they are hungry.

A simple survey can be carried out along a set route, which passes through a variety of habitats. The survey is likely to be more successful if all members of the group are shown pictures of the likely birds to be seen at the start of the route.

DANGER : DO NOT WALK ON THE ICE !

PARK LAKE BIRD SURVEY	Name(s) Jason, Jill + Jim, Date 1ˢᵀ Feb.

Weather conditions −1°c, snow showers.

As you walk around the route, record the symbols on the map to show exactly where you observed each species of bird. Also record the approx. numbers seen (ＨＨＴ = 5).

BIRDS and SYMBOLS	NUMBERS	TOTAL
mallard (m)	ＨＨＴ ⅠⅠⅠⅠ	9
mute swan (ms)	ⅠⅠⅠⅠ	4
canada goose (cg)	ＨＨＴ ＨＨＴ ＨＨＴ ＨＨＴ ＨＨＴ	25
black headed gull (bg)	ＨＨＴ ＨＨＴ ＨＨＴ	15
grey lag goose (gg)	ⅠⅠ	2
coot (c)	ＨＨＴ ＨＨＴ ＨＨＴ ＨＨＴ	20
moorhen (mh)	ⅠⅠⅠ	3
great crested grebe (gcg)	ⅠⅠ	2
crow (cr)	ⅠⅠⅠ	3
song thrush (th)	ⅠⅠ	2
blue tit (bt)	ⅠⅠⅠⅠ	4
robin (r)	Ⅰ	1
wood pigeon (p)	ＨＨＴ Ⅰ	6
magpie (mp)	ⅠⅠⅠ	3

CAR PARK

starlings 12

LAKE

N
W — E
S

0 100 metres

owl

EACH SYMBOL ON THE MAP MAY SHOW A GROUP OF BIRDS

Follow-up Work
Prepare and then compare two graphs:
1. To show the number of each species of bird observed.
2. To show which birds come close to humans and which birds keep a safe distance.

THE ENVIRONMENT

GRASS STUDY

The above **grid map** shows how the different specimens may be recorded in the field. The numbers may be circled on the map to show the most common grass in each grid square. The survey area should include a variety of different environments.

Before the survey, participants may make their own display wallets from pieces of cardboard. This will help to keep the specimens in the order they are collected, as the pockets are numbered according to the map grids. A magnifying lens would be useful for close investigation of the specimens and for identification using a suitable reference book (e.g. *The Observer Book of Grasses, Sedges and Rushes*).

This can be a very pleasant and interesting survey to do in early summer when a variety of grassheads are fully formed. The students may be given a grid map of the survey area, and their job is to collect as many *different* types of grass seed head as possible, and number each different specimen on the grid map. To add a little competition to the exercise 10 points may be awarded for each different species collected, and 50 points for a species that no-one else has found.

(Home made display wallet)

SLOPE STUDY

Suitable footwear will be needed for this study. Only safe slopes should be used. A sketch section of the slope would be useful for the students to record their observations.

Follow-up Work
Make a cardboard model of the slope, with labels, measurements and samples attached to show changes in vegetation, soils, geology, land use and wild life.

STREAM SURVEY

Each team is given a section of stream to survey and map. If possible a clean, safe stream should be chosen with a variety of interesting features. This exercise tends to be more popular in the summer months when the students can paddle around without suffering from cold. Quite an accurate map can be drawn using pace counting or measuring tape for linear distances, and a long cane marked in centimetres for measuring the depth of water at selected points.

The following symbols may be shown on a sketch map of the stream:

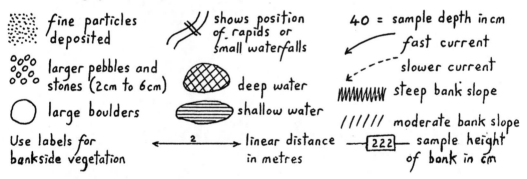

Follow-up Work

1. Make a neat copy of your stream survey map, complete with symbols, key, measurements, labels, colour and date.
2. After a heavy rain storm or flood it is possible that the appearance of your section of the stream could change completely. On an outline of your section of the stream attempt to show how the symbols, measurements and labels could change. Give an explanation.

NOTE: Water pollution could also be an important topic of concern for field studies. Due to obvious health hazards and unpleasant working conditions, any pollution surveys with young people are best done as observations from a distance.

FLOOD RISK

The group may be divided into teams with responsibility for measuring and recording characteristics of the stream and its channel at several points. This survey is mainly intended for lowland streams, where any major rise in water level could result in flood damage to the surrounding area. The survey should only be done when the stream is at a safe level for fieldwork.

Follow-up Work

1. Draw a map of the stream you have studied, and shade blue the area that would be flooded if the stream breached its banks.
2. Make a list of the buildings, roads and land that would be flooded.
3. Calculate the maximum discharge of the stream (at the same recorded velocity) without flooding.

LAND FOR DEVELOPMENT

It is likely that somewhere near to your home plans have been made for a major development which could dramatically affect your environment. Such a development could be a new road, a new factory, a new hypermarket, a new mine, or a new housing estate.

Stage One: A field visit may be arranged to make notes and sketches and to take photographs of the site. These would be useful to help build up opinions about the character and quality of the area.

Stage Two: In preparation for a public inquiry role play exercise each student would need to decide which of the characters they are going to be. Preparation notes should then be made.

Stage Three: The Public Inquiry Role Play Exercise
An appointed chairman would introduce the speakers, give reasons for the public inquiry, and give a final summary. Each spokesperson may have an adviser. Speakers should be prepared to state their case and defend their case if questioned.

AGAINST — FOR

CHAIRMAN

1. J. Smith
(local parish council)
2. A. Heifer
(farmers union)
3. G. Mould
(local cheese dairy)
4. K. Soil
(environmentalist group)
5. Z. Greenfield
(rural protection group)
6. C. Hall
(county council)

7. V. Black
(N.C.B)
8. R. Coal
(energy department)
9. A. Pick
(miners union)
10. O. Job
(employment agency)
11. A. Worker
(local unemployed group)
12. S. Cutter
(mining equipment engineers)

Stage Four: Collect notes, sketches, photographs, maps and newspaper cuttings to make up a scrap book following the progress of the development.
NOTE: Acknowledgement for this exercise is given in this chapter's introductory section.

CANOEING ACTIVITIES

Snake

Raft Crawl

Bulldog

Tag

Canoe Navigation

What's Wrong?

Resuscitation

Situations

Ferry Race

Canoeball

Beginners' Slalom

Skills Relay

Team Rescue

In This Chapter

The games and activities in this chapter have been selected primarily for beginners' groups. Hopefully they will complement the essential skills training common to all beginners' courses, and provide a little controlled fun in a sport which must be very safety conscious.

I have found that beginners tend to improve their canoeing skills when they are in a game situation such as TAG, BULLDOG or CANOEBALL. The games help to provide the motivation, and the newly learned skills are automatically put into operation in the process of chasing after a ball, or avoiding another canoeist in a game of TAG.

There is no substitute however for frequent skills practice sessions with the instructor demonstrating good techniques, while the participants watch and then try out the techniques for themselves. The instructor is always close at hand to offer correction and guidance. These basic training sessions form the basis of beginners' courses, and are especially important for participants who are aiming for the British Canoe Union's (BCU) tests and certificates. A detailed section on Teaching Techniques for Instructors and Coaches is given in the BCU's *Canoeing Handbook*.

This chapter has been arranged so that the easiest games appear towards the beginning, and the more difficult games and exercises appear at the end. The chapter starts with a game called SNAKE which could well fit into ten minutes of the first session of a beginners' course. The participants are given turns at being the leader, who snakes around in his or her canoe, with the other participants trying to follow. This is done at a slow to moderate paddling pace.

Three exercises have been included which could be used for indoor training sessions. These are: WHAT'S WRONG?, RESUSCITATION and SITUATIONS. The intention here is that the visual resources may encourage discussion with instructor and participants. They could also be used as oral or written assessment exercises if appropriate to the course.

I would consider the TEAM RESCUE exercise to be the most difficult in the chapter, if it is to be done quickly and effectively in a deep water capsize situation.

I would like to stress the need for strict supervision and attention to the *'Dos and Don'ts for Canoeists'* which are given in the safety chapter of the BCU's *Canoeing Handbook*. Any group leader or teacher intending to use these games and activities should of course be an experienced and qualified canoeist.

Planning and Safety

Much of the general advice given in Chapter 1 will apply to canoeing activities, however due to the inherent element of risk in this sport, the planning, preparations and safety considerations need to be very thorough.

All staff involved in canoeing activities with beginners' groups should be familiar with the detailed safety guidelines in the BCU's *Canoeing Handbook*, the BCU's current *Safety Check List* (leaflet) and the Canoeing/Safety Afloat sections of *Safety in Outdoor Education*.

The following points briefly identify some of the main concerns:

- Always work well within your own capabilities.
- Allow a staffing ratio of one qualified leader to a maximum of 10 participants for basic canoeing on sheltered enclosed waters, preferably with the help of an experienced assistant.
- Ensure that all participants wear a buoyancy aid or lifejacket of recommended BCU and British Standard, and check that these are correctly fitted.
- Check in advance that participants are confident in water and able to swim 50 metres in normal canoeing clothing.
- Refer to the BCU Coaching Scheme Check List for equipment to be carried and clothing to be worn.
- Always ensure that the leader carries a tow rope and first aid kit.
- Provide helmets (and additional body protection if necessary) for canoeball or canoe polo.
- Inspect each canoe to check that maximum buoyancy is fitted.
- Ensure that bow and stern toggles are fitted.
- Inspect all footrests. The canoeist's foot must not move beyond the footrest or it may become trapped.
- Be sure that the leader's canoe is correctly equipped.
- Check access to water areas with the British Canoe Union.
- Keep an eye open for escape routes if needed.
- Be sure that your level of fitness will allow you to cope efficiently in difficult situations.
- Be on the lookout for weather changes and anticipate the likely effect on your canoeing activities. This particularly applies to breezes and winds.
- Show sound judgement over decisions to go ahead with plans, to cancel if necessary, or to do alternative activities.
- Frequently practice rescue techniques in various situations.
- Know the locations of telephones and emergency services.
- Ensure that all staff/assistants are fully prepared.
- Check the extent of insurance cover.

Qualifications

All instructors/leaders should be trained/qualified in the following:
        RESUSCITATION TECHNIQUES
        LIFE SAVING
        DEEP WATER RESCUE
        FIRST AID

All instructors/leaders will need to refer to the British Canoe Union Coaching Scheme: *Safety Checklist.* The following notes have been extracted directly from the qualifications section.

Leaders of canoe activities should be qualified as follows:

A.   To undertake initial training with beginners, using open cockpit kayaks or canoes only, on placid water only:

        Placid Water Teacher of the British Canoe Union.

B.   To undertake initial 'taster' training with beginners, using closed or open cockpit kayaks or canoes, on very sheltered waters:

        Canoeing Supervisor of the British Canoe Union.
                or
        Trainee Instructor of the British Canoe Union.

C.   To undertake canoeing activities, using closed cockpit kayaks or canoes, on grade 1 water or equivalent sheltered coastal areas only:

        Instructor of the British Canoe Union.

D.   To undertake touring, marathon and sprint racing activities using open cockpit kayaks or canoes only:

        Placid Water Senior Instructor of the British Canoe Union.

E.   To undertake proficiency level expeditioning, grade 2 or above, surfing, or open water canoeing activities:

        Senior Instructor of the British Canoe Union.

Publications, Organisations and Addresses

Safety in Outdoor Education, Dept. for Education, HMSO, 1989
The Water Sports Code, Central Council for Physical Recreation, 1988
British Canoe Union Coaching Scheme
Adbolton Lane, West Bridgford, Nottingham, NG2 5AS
The BCU can provide these publications:
- **Safety Check List** (leaflet), for the guidance of the relevant authorities.
- **Test of Personal Performance and BCU Coaching Awards - Synopsis** (leaflet)
- **Canoeing Handbook: Official Handbook of the British Canoe Union**
        ISBN 0-900082-04-6, 1989
BCU Supplies (catalogue/leaflet) includes inland waterways and river guides plus
numerous other canoeing/kayaking titles. Video titles include teaching and rescue/safety.
Available from: Mobile Adventure Ltd, Bridge Works, Knighton Fields Road West,
Leicester LE2 6LG
Adventure Education (Bookshop and training resources catalogue) includes
canoeing/kayaking titles. Available from: Adventure Education, 39 Brunswick Square,
Penrith, Cumbria CA11 7LS
British Waterways Board
Melbury House, Melbury Terrace, London NW1 6JY
Scottish Canoe Association
Caledonia House, 1 Redheughs Rigg, South Gyle, Edinburgh EH12 9DQ
Welsh Canoeing Association
Pen-y-Bont, Corwen, Clwyd LL21 0EL

SNAKE

SNAKE could well fit into ten minutes of the first session of a beginners' course. The participants are given turns at being the leader, who snakes around in his or her canoe, with the other participants trying to follow. This is done at a slow to moderate paddling pace.

RAFT CRAWL

Most canoe instructors would show participants how to 'raft up' the canoes (See sketch below.) at an early stage in their course. This provides stability in open water, and gives beginners a feeling of security. An interesting development is to have a raft crawl race. Each participant in turn climbs out of their canoe, crawls along the front of the canoe raft and then back along the back of the raft to return to their own place. The instructor starts to time each participant when satisfied that everyone is holding the raft firmly together.

NOTE:
1. In windy conditions the raft will soon drift away, therefore the instructor would obviously need to be alert for any hazards.
2. Participants should realise that the canoes can be easily damaged if anyone attempts to walk or run along the canoe raft.

BULLDOG

To play 'canoe bulldog', a chosen participant is positioned in the middle of a river, facing the rest of the group who are lined up along one bank. When the instructor gives the signal to start, the rest of the group try to paddle past the middle person (within set boundaries) to reach the opposite river bank. The middle person aims to touch as many people as possible on the arm or body, with his or her paddle blade. This is done gently! As soon as anyone is touched, then they help to prevent others from passing. The instructor gives the signal for each crossing to start, only when satisfied that everyone is in position. Several crossings may be needed before everyone is touched by a paddle.

Safety
Before anyone starts, all participants should understand that if anyone capsizes, then the others should immediately come to help.

TAG

In this variation of 'tag' the players leave their paddles on the bank side, and only use their hands for propulsion. When one player has been touched, he or she then helps to tag the others. Another alternative which will test participants' balancing skills, is to play the same game with legs hanging outside the canoe.

CANOE NAVIGATION

This exercise is similar to LEADING IN TURN in Chapter 3 in that each participant is given responsibility for navigating and leading the group for a given leg of the route. The instructor would need to prepare several large scale waterproof maps with check points circled and numbered. Members of the canoe group would benefit from a practice session in setting a map and setting a compass bearing from a map before the canoe navigation exercise. The instructor accompanies the canoe group around the course to give guidance and to assess the performance of each student leader.

WHAT'S WRONG?

What should be the correct way?

RESUSCITATION

Any canoeist would benefit from learning basic first aid techniques. A drowning situation is always a remote possibility, therefore training in artificial resuscitation is a valuable aspect of any canoeing course. Detailed guidelines on artificial resuscitation are given in *First Aid: The Authorised Manual of St. John Ambulance Association and Brigade*, and in the British Canoe Union's *Canoeing Handbook*.

SITUATIONS

Situations such as this and those shown on the next page are intended as discussion points for instructors and participants.

A suggested method for an indoor training session would be to prepare a set of cards for use in the procedure described below.

Each card would cover one situation. Some of the ideas shown on the next page may be used, depending on the experience of the group. Other relevant situations could include decisions that participants could realistically be expected to face.

Procedure
1. Split the group into twos or threes.
2. Allow ten minutes to discuss the alternative plans of action for the first situation card. Participants should try to agree on the best course of action and be prepared to justify their answer.
3. Exchange cards several times, repeating the above procedure.
4. Finally, bring everyone together to listen to other responses to the situations. The leader/instructor would try to acknowledge any positive answers. If an acceptable response has not been given, then the instructor/leader will need to give their personal answer, preferably with reference to real situations.

An alternative way to use this exercise is to print the situations with illustrations onto transparencies for use with an overhead projector.

What would YOU do in these situations? Give your reasons.

① Your friend's canoe hits a rock and starts to sink. You are ten miles from the nearest village, and half way along a fast flowing river in the Scottish Highlands.

② A speed boat has just whizzed past your beginners' group in the middle of Lake Windermere. The waves from the boat have caused two children to capsize.

③ Your canoe group drives past an inviting stretch of river which unfortunately is private. Most of the group would like to stop and do some canoeing.

PRIVATE

④

One member of your canoe group starts to show signs of suffering from hypothermia. You are only three miles from the finish of a twenty mile team race along the River Tees, on a cold December morning.

⑤

A group of experienced canoeists have canoed along a stretch of the Yorkshire coast. As they approach their destination they find that there is no easy way into shore. Very large breakers are pounding onto the beach, and a dangerous looking swell is visible at the pier. The only safe landing point is three miles along the coast.

FERRY RACE

The aim of this game is to see which team can ferry their passenger across a lake and return to the same point in the shortest time. A distance of about fifty metres is adequate for each journey. Each team has three people (including one passenger) two canoes, and one paddle. Each team member should change positions at the halfway point. The passenger should not stand on the canoes as this could easily cause damage. This game is obviously intended for a warm, sunny day in summer, as the passenger could end up in the water.

Safety
Buoyancy aids should be worn by all participants.

CANOEBALL

The basic idea is that two teams aim to score a goal with a plastic football by passing it by hand between members of the team. Goalposts may be improvised on each bank side, or just one goal may be used if necessary. A player must not hold the ball for more than three seconds. The paddle may only be used to manoeuvre the canoe, to intercept the ball in the air, or to reach the ball on the water. The referee may award a free throw for infringements of the rules. The ball is thrown in by the non-offending team if the ball goes out of the play area.

NOTE: Players should be penalised for dangerous use of the paddle.

Variations
1. The game can also be played very successfully without paddles.
2. The game may be played without goals, in the middle of a lake or river, although the aim in this case would be for each team to keep possession of the ball for as long as possible, by passing the ball between members of the team.

Value fun
manoeuvring skills
sporting spirit
determination.

confidence
team effort
challenging activity

NOTE: This exercise is based on the very popular game 'Canoe Polo', further details of which are given in the BCU's *Canoeing Handbook*.

BEGINNERS' SLALOM

A beginners' slalom training course can be set up fairly quickly, using long canes or posts which are pushed into the lake or river bed. Some of the problems set on top class slalom courses can also be used on still or slow moving water, offering the beginners a chance to test out their skills in a controlled situation. As in top class competitions, all competitors would be timed on a stop watch.

② Turn and reverse through narrow gate.

① Manoeuvre forwards between narrow gates.

③ Turn and draw stroke across to forward gate.

④ Limbo.

⑤ Throw the paddle over high gate, collect paddle and sprint to the finish line.

Safety
Even on a simple training course such as this there are likely to be many capsizes. All participants should therefore have practised the capsize drill before this session.

SKILLS RELAY

This is a useful way of assessing basic canoeing skills towards the end of a beginners' course. Two relay teams line up on the bank with their canoes ready. When the instructor gives the signal to start, the first person in each team carries his or her canoe to the water and performs the techniques shown below. The other members of each relay team then follow on in turn to complete the same techniques. The first relay team to complete all techniques to a satisfactory standard is the winner. The instructor may prefer to use a scoring system so that each technique is awarded points.

① Launching and embarking using a draw stroke.

② 360° turn using a sweep stroke.

③ Forward paddling.

④ Emergency stop.

⑤ Backward paddling.

⑥ Support stroke on both sides.

(This one didn't work!)

⑦ Coming alongside and disembarking.

TEAM RESCUE

When participants have progressed beyond the elementary stages of canoeing, they should begin to learn various rescue techniques. The team exercise below shows a very stable method of emptying an upturned kayak in deep water. Notice that the person in the water helps to lift or lower his kayak when required. When the kayak has been emptied the capsized canoeist may reach across as shown in stage two below, and then quickly slide his feet down into the kayak.

Stage One: Rafting together and emptying the kayak over the two hulls.

Stage Two: Re-entry.

NOTE: A detailed section on deep water rescue techniques is given in the British Canoe Union's *Canoeing Handbook*.

OTHER OUTDOOR ACTIVITIES

By Alan Dearling and Alan Smith

In This Chapter

In this chapter we have pulled together a number of very different activities which do not fall easily within the previous chapter groupings. Some of them, such as EARTH MAGIC, HASH RUNNING or OFF-ROAD MOTORCYCLING may be new to many group leaders. Others take familiar activities and either give them a novel twist or suggest ways in which they can be used in the youth training context, e.g. GONE FISHING, ON THE BEACH or IN THE POOL.

Working with young people should be fun and stimulating for both them and their leaders. We hope that some of these ideas will increase the variety of activities and hence the fun.

Our first example is EARTH MAGIC...

Many people testify to the feelings and power that ancient sites still hold. As an exercise with young people, ley-hunting or just seeking out sites of antiquity can be a fascinating introduction to archaeology, and also the modern preoccupation with ancient wisdom and legends.

EARTH MAGIC

No, I'm not recommending turning all your youth group into magicians!

Young people, like many adults, are fascinated by myths, legends and places of special significance. Large numbers of well-respected academics and historians have written weighty books about the significance of particular sites and the 'power' of places. These sites can also be a source of learning and wonderment for youth groups and can provide an unusual focus for a trek through the country.

There are a number of good guides to interesting sites. Janet and Colin Bord have written *The Secret Country* and *Mysterious Britain* (both in Paladin). Jacquetta Hawkes: *Guide to Prehistoric and Roman Monuments* (Cardinal) and Nicholas Thomas: *Guide to Prehistoric England* (Batsford) along with Francis Hitching: *Earth Magic* are valuable sources of places to investigate and learn about.

Stone circles, menhirs and dolmens are of special interest and tantalise succeeding generations who look for their 'meaning'. Alfred Watkins proposed a theory that many of these old sites are situated on lines of power, which may also be ancient trackways. Identifying these 'ley lines' can be a wonderful exercise for young people, whether or not they actually believe in Watkin's theory.

Procedure
In its simplest form, ley line hunters use a large scale map and try to identify ancient points which are in a straight line with each other. If there are three or more in a line, most usually with one just in sight of the next, then this might just be a ley line or ancient track! Modern followers of the theory also look for:
- Castles and forts.
- Ancient wells.
- Beacons.
- Burial mounds, tumuli and cairns.
- Moats and islands.
- Old churches and abbeys.
- Old cross roads that are named: these may have special 'mark stones' situated there, which often have old notches and inscriptions on them.
- Old stone crosses have also survived in a number of locations.

Again, these are first checked on a map using a ruler to check for alignments, and then they are visited as a piece of active field-research to see if anything of significance such as old stones, signs of old tracks or other ruins exist on the line.

RIVER TREKS

An activity which takes a bit of planning, but which can be lots of fun and instructive is sourcing a stream or river.

Procedure

The idea is a simple one. With your group, use a map to identify the source of a local river or stream. Then the task is to organise a 'quest' or 'adventure' to find the source and then, if time permits, to follow all or some of the route to the mouth.

Points worth noting:
- You will need the Pathfinder Ordnance Survey maps, two and a half inches to the mile for the route.
- If you want to keep close to the river bed, you will need to get permission of landowners on the route.
- If you are going to camp, you will need to ensure that all members of the party have the necessary equipment. Keep the equipment as light as possible, perhaps using the selection of items as a useful group exercise in its own right.
- Keep in touch with someone back at base, with agreed times to phone in and keep them informed of your progress and target destinations.

Alternative Ideas

I have also been involved with a group which ran the length of a river as a relay-challenge, and another which took canoes and mountain bikes in support vehicles, and used a local pony-trek stable for horses to enable the group to experience as many modes of travel as possible.

ON THE BEACH

Staff often take youth groups to the seaside or to the more challenging coastal paths and cliffs of Britain. Other organisations are situated close to the seashore and the creative possibilities it offers.

Safety
As with other activities, make sure that you give some clear and appropriate guidelines for safety in the area you are using, such as:
- Take care not to get cut off by rising tides.
- Stay away from cliffs, landslips, mudflows and quicksand.
- Many parts of beaches are rough, with sharp stones and boulders. Good solid footwear is required.
- Do not go in the sea unless you have specifically been given permission.
- Take care on many of the rocks and boulders as they are slippery with seaweed.
- Do not disturb living creatures.

Activities
These can take many forms. On the next page are ideas for two:
Beachcombing
Beach clean-up

Beachcombing

All sorts of objects end up being left or washed up on the beach. This can be utilised as a group activity. I would recommend getting your group to work in pairs. Give them a set time to collect items in, then the whole group can compare how many items they have found and the range of items. This can be turned into a competition if you like, but it is rather difficult to judge!

The range of items I have found with groups includes old coins, unusual seashells, fossils, old glass and china, including whole bottles, dead fish, bits of boats and even part of a shark's jaw!

Alternatively, you might wish to organise a specific hunt for:
> *fossils*
> *rocks and minerals*
> *seashells*

On many UK beaches there are an amazing variety of all three. Ammonites, crinoids and belemnites are three common types of fossil, while there are five common types of shells: gastropods, bivalves, cephalopods, chions and scaphopoda. Usborne's small spotter's guides to shells, rocks and minerals are useful resources, as are the equally well-presented Letts pocket guides to fossils, rocks and minerals.

Beach clean-up

Increasingly, ecological issues are being addressed with direct action, and rubbish on the shoreline is both an eyesore and a potential health hazard. Given gloves and strong collecting sacks, young people can quite easily be encouraged into taking part in beach clean-ups. It can be turned into either a sponsored event for one of the eco-charities such as Friends of the Earth or Greenpeace, or organised as a small, group competition.

The Marine Conservation Society and Readers' Digest organise a nation-wide beach survey and clean-up each autumn, and are always keen to hear from groups wanting to help in their area. Contact: The Local Groups Officer, Marine Conservation Society, 9 Gloucester Road, Ross-on-Wye, Herefordshire HR9 5BU. Telephone: 01989 566017. They provide a detailed instruction pack on how to organise the event and what safety precautions need to be considered.

IN THE POOL

Safety

Safety in the water is of paramount importance. Organising events for swimmers and non-swimmers in a swimming pool or in the sea is a mixture of common-sense, a sharp eye, quick wits and enough personal skill in life saving techniques to be able to act swiftly if any participant shows signs of being in trouble. It is also important for the organiser to have a basic understanding of first aid, including mouth to mouth resuscitation, and have buoyancy aids on hand. In the sea, a lifebelt with a line attached is very useful.

Water Games

Water games can be tremendous fun and provide an opportunity for learning through play. A few possible games are included here which are ideal for groups of youngsters of varying swimming abilities and ages. NOTE: An adult organiser with recognised swimming and life-saving qualifications should always be on hand.

Jaws

This is a water-based tag game. To start with, one player volunteers, or is chosen to be the shark. All the other players are in the water holding on to the edges. The organiser yells 'Shark Attack' and everyone must try to reach the opposite side of the pool without being touched (eaten) by the shark. Variations include, everyone 'eaten' must leave the pool, or becomes a shark for the next round. Another alternative is to set a time limit for the shark attack, say five minutes, during which, players try to make as many crossings of the width of the pool as possible. Any player touching the pool-sides is usually deemed safe.

Corkers!

This involves the games organiser throwing a good number of corks into the pool (clean ones!) and the participants try to collect as many as they can in a set amount of time. The game can be played as individuals, pairs or teams.

Float racing

Many young people have their own polystyrene float to help them learn to use their arms and legs properly. Outdoor and indoor pools can also often supply them for use by youth groups. The floats are a good piece of equipment for a relay race. Teams are chosen, with one float per team. Each team member must swim a length or width of the pool either holding on to the float with their hands, and using leg power, or grasping the float between their thighs and using only arm strokes. They hand their float on to the next member of the relay team for the next leg of the race. It's good fun and helps give young people confidence in their swimming.

Crossing the Divide

The idea in this game is to allow all participants to cross a given stretch of water in any way they wish as long as it is different from the method used by their colleagues. Players take turns to cross the pool or swim between two markers, and if played in shallow water, non-swimmers can take part by hopping, walking backwards, or any other method they can devise.

GONE FISHING

Since fishing is the UK's most popular outdoor activity after walking, it seems only sensible to include it in this book. As the 1990s progress, resistance to fishing as a sport on ethical grounds increases, but many view it as acceptable, especially sea fishing where most larger fish can provide a vitamin and protein-full source of food.

Fishing can be a solitary or a group activity. It can take place on lakes, rivers, inland waterways or in the sea. Fishing can be undertaken using varying lengths and types of rods and reels and hand lines from riverbanks, bridges, boats, harbour walls or by beach casting.

At its most complex, it is an expensive, equipment intensive sport, but there is still a very real chance of a twelve year old with ten pounds worth of second hand gear from the local fishing shop making the catch of the day.

Rules
The rules governing freshwater fishing are very different and more stringent than those for sea fishing. Almost all freshwater fishing requires a licence, and in competitions there are very specific rules for the weight of fish which are kept alive in a 'keep net' whilst smaller fish are put back. Check with your local fishing shop for the regulations, charges and places to fish.

Safety

If you or your youth group are fishing in the sea, knowing the tide conditions is essential. In some parts of Britain you can trek miles, literally, at low tide to reach a shallow ripple of the sea's edge - no use for fishing at all! Also be safety conscious, and take local advice on:

- weather conditions;
- any dangerous cliffs;
- points where you might get cut off by the tide;
- if you are using a boat, ensure that someone on land knows where you are going and when you are due back. Take flares, a whistle and most importantly, life jackets.

Competition

Using fishing as an activity with a group of young people can be a casual affair, or can be organised into an informal competition. This may be judged singly or working in teams. Fishing competitions are usually organised for a fixed period, for instance two to four hours. Caught fish are kept under the water in a flexible tubing of net called a keep net. At the end of the competition, the winner is the person with greatest weight of fish, rather than greatest number, so the organiser needs a set of scales available to judge the contest.

Equipment

The organiser may need to hire rods, reels, lines and other equipment to organise such an event, so some charge may need to be made to participants. A knife, spare hooks, line and weights are among the other necessities. The bait required and size of hook used, weights, traces and floats all depend on what the angler is trying to catch. For instance, spinners are used for mackerel fishing in the sea, and flies and feathers are used to entice many freshwater fish. Bread, maggots, small pieces of fish and worms are all used for bait. There are many good inexpensive books from which you can easily learn the basics.

Value

Many young people enjoy fishing, but have no-one to show them the fundamental skills required. It is quite likely that organising a fishing event will lead to some individuals continuing to learn about and participate in the sport.

A spin-off value of fishing is that it often introduces young people to their local natural heritage, whether it is the canalside in Birmingham or the southern coastal bays. Along with this can come the acquisition of knowledge and understanding of wildlife, the forces of nature and the local flora and fauna. All very much part of working outdoors with young people!

AFLOAT ON THE WATERWAYS

Many organisers of youth groups have found that Britain's heritage of canals and rivers offer an ideal setting for an unusual and stimulating outdoor experience.

The waterways were principally developed as an alternative to moving cargo by road. They had their heyday before steam power enabled the development of the railways. What is left is a maze of navigable routes which provide an ideal resource for holiday transportation and for the more adventurous water-borne traveller.

Value
For youth groups, the canal-boat experience is nearly ideal. It can offer:
- An introduction to Britain's industrial history as well as a back door to some of the most beautiful and unspoilt areas of rural Britain.
- A group living and working experience, where planning routes, meal preparation, steering, navigating, mooring the boat, and working locks are all an integral part.
- An opportunity to explore and live in a changing countryside and to learn about the wildlife and natural history of the waterways, banks and surrounding areas.

Activities
A typical week's itinerary could involve:
- Travelling about 80 miles.
- Opening, operating and navigating up to 100 locks. Winching paddles open and opening lock gates works up a healthy appetite!
- Teamwork, with everyone fulfilling a number of roles and generally 'mucking in.'

Boats
The most common narrow boats, often incorrectly called 'barges' are usually just under seven foot wide and can be up to seventy-two feet long. They can be simply fitted out and equipped, or offer near luxury surroundings including central heating, calor gas cooker, TV, fridge and shower. Toilets are always a bit of a problem, as the holding tank fills up and needs emptying! They can accommodate between 4 and 12 people in bunks or on convertible lounge beds. Moorings can usually be found beside the towpath, and shops and other facilities are available in villages and towns.

Specially converted boats for people with disabilities and special needs also exist and these are frequently equipped with hydraulic ramps for wheelchairs.

Planning
Several important issues are addressed in Chapter 1. Some special considerations apply if you are considering taking a youth group afloat:
- Take time to visit the boat you are hiring in advance.
- Do some research about hire rates, what it includes, especially in terms of insurance and breakages.
- Learn a bit about how the boat works and possible routes.
- Involve members of your group in the preparation.

Choosing a hire company
Choose a hire company which is sympathetic to the needs of youth groups. If they build and maintain their own fleet, they will be likely to offer a better service than companies who rent out other people's boats for a service fee. Check if they provide a bit of basic training in how to work and maintain the boat. They may even be able to provide special equipment such as additional canoes and lifejackets.

Publications, organisations and addresses
For further information try looking at a copy of *Waterways World* magazine, or contacting one of these organisations:

Inland Waterways Association
114 Regent's Park Rd
London NW1 8UQ

The British Waterways Board Information Centre
Melbury House
Melbury Terrace
London NW1 6JX.

HASH RUNNING

This was developed in the Far East by British servicemen and workers. A gentleman called Gisbert was the original hasher. Since then it has been re-imported to the U.K. and every other part of the world. In the British Isles there are many clubs, often called the such and such Hash House Harriers (sometimes shortened to H3). My co-author, Alan, belonged to the Malvern Hash in Worcestershire and still runs the occasional hash run in Dorset and Devon.

So, what is it all about?

The basic idea has evolved from the paper chase, but is much better for mixed ability running groups, and more ecologically sound!

Procedure
To organise a hash event, a volunteer agrees to lay one or more hash trails from a given starting point, usually a country pub or sports clubhouse, where the 'hashers' will gather at a pre-arranged time. The trail is marked with small piles of sand, flour or sawdust on tracks, paths and roadways. These are usually placed at fairly regular intervals, say every hundred metres. The faster runners follow the trail until they come to a 'check' sign with arrows pointing in several directions. This denotes a number of choices, and the lead runners share the task of 'checking' perhaps three or four trails which have been laid from the intersection point. Tradition is that they call back "On! On!" to the runners

behind them when they've found a continuous trail. This message is relayed back through the pack. If uncertain they call back "Checking!"' and "On two!", "On three!" etc., But only one trail is correct and after a few hundred metres the runners on the false trails will find themselves confronted with a sawdust 'X', and they yell "False trail!" or "Check back!" They then have to run back to the intersection and pick up the correct trail. Eventually the trail returns the hashers back to the starting point, with the leader calling an "On home!" instruction.

NOTE: Whenever there is a main road intersection, or after a longish stretch, the hash organiser marks the ground with an 'H' or 'R', which means "Hold!" or "'Halt!" or "Re-group!" This allows all the hash participants to re-group, and allows a safety check to see that no-one has gone missing.

Everyone can join in!
It is the false trails that act as the balancing factor since they ensure that the lead runners do extra mileage, and it gives the proverbial 'tortoise' the chance to catch up with the 'hare'.

Quite often, the organiser will set short and long trails, of perhaps four and eight miles, which allow the runners with extra stamina to put in extra miles, whilst providing a more leisurely course for the less experienced, or there may be 'approved' short cuts. No map reading is used, and most hash clubs are a mix of wizened veteran runners, young teenagers, dogs, keep fit enthusiasts and a scattering of serious athletes who understand the training value of hash running across country. All in all it is a very sociable form of running.

Value
For groups of young people it can offer a good mixture of country path rambling, running and companionable fun. As long as the organiser has a good knowledge of footpaths and bridleways and keeps away from main roads, this can provide a couple of hours healthy outdoor entertainment.

Planning and Safety
1. It is best that the hash organiser runs with the hash to ensure that folk do not get horribly lost, possibly because a mark has been obliterated. It is useful to have a reliable back marker who can act as sweeper.
2. In fields where there are a lot of young cattle or sheep, the runners may need to slow down or walk to avoid panicking the livestock. It is important that the organiser should warn landowners of the event in advance.
3. Especially on hot days or evenings, it is a good idea if the organiser sets up a drinks container and paper cups at one of the halts at about the half way point. Sweating can cause quite bad dehydration.
4. If the organiser puts on a bum bag they can carry a whistle, a small first aid kit and a map, all of which may prove useful.
5. Hashers should always follow the Country Code, particularly shutting gates.
6. Laying a trail is great fun, but requires map reading skills and a desire to out guess the faster runners!
7. Someone should have responsibility for car keys or leave them with someone at the base.
8. A good hash route will take in lots of different types of terrain, preferably including mud and some water!

Tradition

Part of the fun of hashing is its quirky rules and traditions! Often the organising committee have distinctive titles: Grand Master, Grand Mistress, Hash Cash, On Sec, Religious Advisor and Hash Horn. Individual hashers also gain Hash Handles, which are not always too complimentary!

Hash Runners are particularly active in fund raising for charities. They also organise local events and runs, print up special T-shirts and are increasingly family orientated. Every two years there is a UK Nash (National) Hash gathering, where many trails are set and much celebration takes place. This includes alternative Hash events such as 'Wibbly Wobbly' races and 'Down Downs'.

Altogether, it's about having FUN above all else.

OFF-ROAD MOTOR-CYCLING

Off-road motor cycling, together with banger racing, has been increasingly used by social work, probation and community education groups as an exciting and character building outdoor activity for young people. A number of groups exist throughout the UK to promote non-competitive and competitive riding, concentrating on many different aspects from trail and trial riding through to off-road side-car riding. .

Value
The use of motorcycles in social groupwork programmes has grown considerably in the last fifteen years. Professionals from a number of disciplines have begun to realise that it can provide a successful method of engaging young people in an alternative to offending and vandalism. It offers a unique blend of:
- skills training
- control and discipline
- excitement

In a number of projects such as RUTS in Scotland the accent has been on integrating trials riding and bike maintenance into a groupwork programme which is run by a mix of volunteers and professionals, many of whom come to the project as bikers and help to break down the model of social worker meddling, which many deprived and abused young people have. The two activities also offer a variety of opportunities which are both exciting, and perceived of as adult by young people, which many groupwork activities certainly are not.

Gender issues are especially interesting to explore as macho young males can find young women more able in trials riding. It certainly can provide a useful test of stereotypes.

Planning and Safety
In this book, I cannot go into all the complications of running a successful and safe motor project, but the following are some of the key considerations. Consideration of this list will help anyone even remotely thinking about entering into the fairly new world of motorcycle youth work.
1. Get advice on the most appropriate machinery for the intended users. Trials bikes, for instance, are likely to be more suitable than trails bikes.
2. Be sure to obtain permission to use land. Think of contacting the local council , local forestry authority, large agricultural landowners, development companies.
3. Get proper insurance cover.
4. Keep the bikes properly maintained.
5. Select and train an appropriate staff group. Experience has shown that all staff, including the professional social workers or teachers, must be able to ride bikes to some degree. Inevitably they must also have a sense of humour when the young people pull their leg as the adult leader keeps falling off!
6. Create a balanced programme integrating games, discussion, feedback, training and riding skills, maintenance, video interviews and role plays.

Consider whether it is better to start a new off-road project or buy into another project's resources and expertise. The RUTS project is amongst the most experienced, having been funded from Lothian Regional Council to work with young people from both community education and social work. If interested I would suggest that you contact them:

> RUTS
> 11 Arthur Street
> Leith
> Edinburgh
> Scotland
> EH6 5DA
> (031) 553 6021

> **or**

> The National Association of Motor Projects
> 14 Chetwood Rd
> Tadworth
> Surrey
> KT20 5PW
> (0737) 352567

This is the co-ordinating body for many statutory and voluntary motor projects, ranging from karts and bikes up to stock cars. Their funding comes from a variety of sources including the Probation Service and the Home Office.

Happy and safe biking!!!

OTHER ACTIVITIES